RIVERS OF MEMORY

RIVERS OF MEMORY

A Journey on Maine's Historic Midcoast Waterways

JOHN GIBSON

WITH PHOTOGRAPHS BY THE AUTHOR

MAPS BY RUTH ANN HILL

DOWN EAST BOOKS

Cover photograph by John Gibson

ISBN: 0-89272-651-2
LCCN: 2003113886

Book design by Harrah Lord, Yellow House Studio
Printed at Versa Press, E. Peoria, Ill.

2 4 5 3 1

Down East Books
A division of Down East Enterprise, Inc.,
publisher of *Down East*, the Magazine of Maine

Book orders: 1-800-685-7962
www.downeastbooks.com

Remembering
John Edward Gibson
and
Bessie Hanson Gibson

Books by John Gibson

50 Hikes in Maine

Walking the Maine Coast

Go Light

Walking the New England Coast

50 Hikes in Coastal and Southern Maine

Maine's Most Scenic Roads: 25 Routes Off the Beaten Path

New Hampshire's Most Scenic Roads: 22 Routes Off the Beaten Path

The Traveler's Guide to the Most Scenic Roads In Massachusetts

Weekend Walks on the New England Coast

Rivers of Memory

Contents

An early postcard view of the St. George, before 1910.
Courtesy of the Warren Historical Society.

A river is the most human and companionable of inanimate things.

It has a life, a character, a voice of its own. . . .

For real company and friendship, there is nothing outside

of the animal kingdom that is comparable to a river.

—Henry Van Dyke, *Little Rivers*

PREFACE

Who has never wanted to get up one morning to disappear to some favored place out of earshot of the world? To head out on the current, finding the sun on the water, the breeze at your back and some welcoming place waiting upstream, or to beat downriver, stroking easily with the tide to those places where the land yields finally to the rushing sea? Along Maine's coastal rivers, these sentiments are commonplace and as fresh as the tide. They are a reason for going.

For centuries, Maine's coastal rivers offered a bosom of settlement in America's earliest hours, a source of timber for hulls and masts, and a pooling place for the fish that filled the offshore nets of ships of many nations. These rivers became the arteries not only of settlement, but also of moving timber, masts, barrels, cloth, brick, fuel, tar, and dozens of other commodities. Along their shores arose villages that became small towns or cities, an established Indian culture retreating in the face of armed European occupation.

The legacy of early American community building still exists here in the villages and towns along the rivers. Architecture unique to these places lingers. One still hears legends of the seagoing and shipbuilding world that embraced the coast and its rivers. Fish ladders, old mill sites, the remnants of the frozen water industry, shipways, the dams that still exist or that have gone away and the forests that have returned in many places: each attests to the culture of an earlier America. From the rivers, one can almost reach out and touch it all.

This summer, after a winter of housebound discontent, I decided to take to some of Maine's essential rivers and to find my way in their channels, islands, and eddies. I would spare a week and follow rivers to where they narrowed and became one with their surroundings. Along the way, I would sample certain upriver towns, investigate old fortifications, skirt falls, and, most important, acquaint myself with the Maine world as seen from her rivers. A fine madness descends occasionally, and I was prepared to follow it.

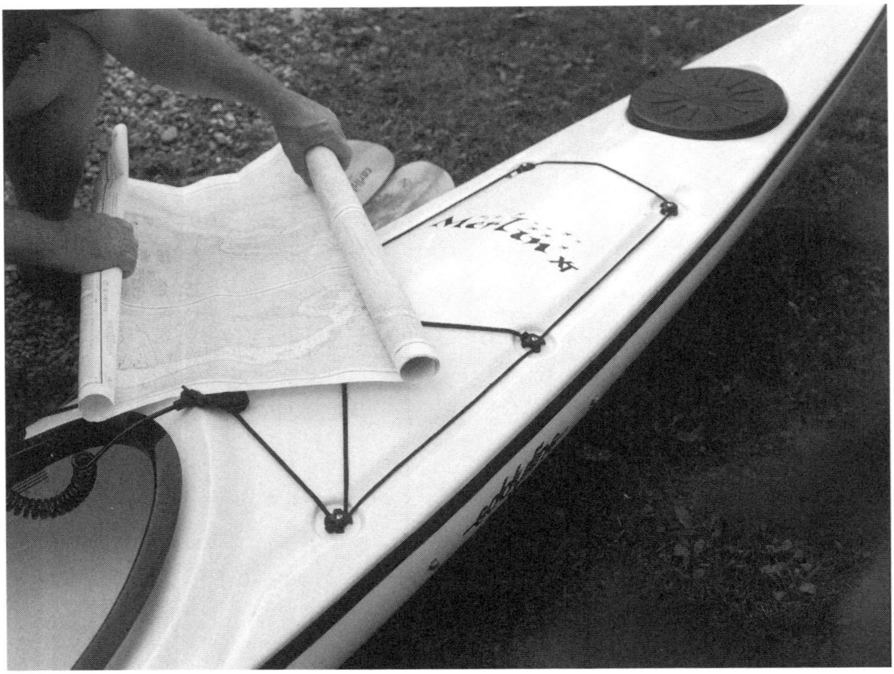

PHOTOGRAPH BY DIANNA RUST

A kayak was readied, maps studied, tide charts reckoned with, and histories consulted. This was going to be a journey of out-of-the-way places, each with a debt to the rivers I would travel and each with its own memories of the life that had been lived there. My aim, too, was to get the feel of these waters, to see what the back doors of river towns had to show me, and to enjoy the woodsy shore as it unrolled. In Maine, rivers emerge everywhere, but then disappear rapidly, secluded as they are in forests, out behind pastures, and in the beds they have made for themselves in hidden lowlands. These rivers are spotted from rural roads as one drives along, but they pull away shortly, and the passing thought is "Now where does that go?" I proposed to find out for myself.

I blocked out a week on my calendar, inspired, certainly, by Thoreau's week-long journey on the Concord and Merrimack rivers in Massachusetts, a trip made more than a century and a half ago in a boat of the Thoreau brothers' own making. I had no heroic notion of journeying, my interest in headlines such as "He Conquers the Rapids and Beats Danger" being nil. When heroics are the goal, one doesn't get to see much of anything, actually. I hoped to see a great deal, both past and present, living and remembered. This would be a leisurely journey responsive only to that tyrannical timekeeper, the tide, interrupted, if at all, only by darkness and weather. Distance was left to how much river I could cover in the week allotted.

Thoreau opined that we get used to viewing the regional landscape, wherever we reside, so that it gradually becomes invisible to us. He suggested that if we move a little amidst the familiar landscape and look at our surroundings anew, something will be revealed to us. I set out to do just that, to grow a little wiser about my own neck of the woods, to give myself a geography lesson, and to come home satisfied.

Early one morning I arrived at the first of the rivers I would travel, slid my boat into the water, and headed north. What follows are my minutes of the meeting, all the sessions of which I hope you will attend.

John Gibson

BEGINNINGS

It is these comparatively cheap and private expeditions that substantiate our existence and batten our lives—as, where a vine touches the earth in its undulating course, it puts forth roots and thickens its stock. Our employment generally is tinkering, mending the old, worn-out teapot of society. . . . Better for me, says my genius, to go cranberrying this afternoon for the Vaccinium oxycoccus *in Gowing's Swamp, to get but a pocketful and learn its peculiar flavor—aye, and the flavor of Gowing's Swamp and of life in New England. . . .*

—Henry David Thoreau, *Wild Fruits* (1859)

The river slides inward, sleek, black, and in a hurry, its surface shiny like veined, polished marble. Little whirling pools, hints of submerged activity, roil like an artist's decorative line along its dark surface as an advancing current scours the hidden bottom. Across the river, from the east, dawn occurs as an intense, spreading glow behind staggered hardwoods. Though late summer has begun to lose its grip, the air rises warm, even fragrant. Officially, the sun will not fully appear for another half hour, but day advances well enough.

Standing in water in a little cove below Dodge Point, I survey the river south of me, those lower reaches of the Damariscotta which at certain hours thread toward the open seas, draining whole regions above Maine's rock-lodged coastal web. Lobstermen are absent at this hour, perhaps gone out to haul already, and pleasure boaters are, surely, caught on the ledges of sleep. For now, the river is a moving ribbon of quiet, surging tide. It is a deceiving quiet; one would do well to accord respect to this incoming flood. Its polished exterior masks boundless muscle.

Not far south of here, out beyond the Cuckolds, lie the outposts and islands where white men began European settlement of the Americas. Places that go unmentioned in the comical history books purveyed in the nation's public schools. Places of raw beginning fed by rivers such as the Damariscotta. Here, too, is as good a corner as any for a restless sort with a fine little boat to begin a journey upriver, following the ghosts of those who navigated here four hundred years ago.

Maine's middle coast is a territory of rivers. Live here long enough, and those rivers slowly, progressively take hold of one and connect. They are the unifying, persistent leitmotif of whole regions. Commerce, village life, the natural world follow their course. Human activities dissolve, disappear, and reconstitute, but these waters continue their embrace. In rivers lie the truths of a place, a region, a nation. The Damariscotta is no exception. All of history and human experience follow water.

Not far upstream, Dodge Point catches the first light, a line of yellow gold forming across the red pine treetops in this lovely, wooded conifer plantation. I busy myself with the kayak, arranging those few things I deem necessary, putting lunch in the forward hatch and my pump and paddle float under the bungees aft of the cockpit. A change of dry clothes finds a place in the larger, rear hatch. I secure a water bottle next to the seat and, for now, leave a paddle propped against the hull. There is a comfortable ritual about such things, an order of practice, of getting ready, that is slow, measured, reassuring; a ritual of departure far older than any of us now living.

The early hour brings a certain pleasure, like receiving the gift of something new, spotless, unsullied. This hour also offers a desirable rising tide, which will add support to my upriver journey and carry me over the submerged ledges that await above the nearest village. A boater can cover distance on these rivers irrespective of tides, of course, but at a price exacted in both speed and effort—and, sometimes, safety. Since I will be the sole engine of my own ascent, capturing the thrust of the tide justifies an early beginning, the pre-dawn water cool and vacant as the sky grows lighter and the day goes on making.

The river I will climb begins far inland, feeds a grand lake of the same name, Damariscotta, then waters a broad, shallow bay before heading in a southerly direction. Great Salt Bay, a perennially windswept expanse, empties its contents, both fresh and tidal, into the lower Damariscotta, finally running to the sea. The river makes its presence known in dozens of hidden coves, and one can travel the back roads here, idly tracing the course of this or other rivers through tiny, hidden communities.

For the curious, entire days evaporate in pursuit of riverine bays, inlets, falls, rapids, and islands where Maine's rivers meld and divide. Forever bound up with each waterside town's history and reason for being, these rivers were a conduit for establishment in an era long before roads existed. In the name of practicality, human enterprise and human settlement have intimately attached themselves to these midcoast waters, large and small, as persistently as whelks on rock. The very origins of American seaborne commerce reside in the tangle of bays, harbors, and inlets of which this river is a part. Water is its own excuse.

I haul my sleek little boat off the shingle, its brilliant white reflecting back the low, early light. *Merlin* is its name, and its finely conceived hull will ride many miles of river water before the week is out if we, *Merlin* and I, are dealt no surprises. We are not impulsive types. Our journey really began last winter in the kind of ruminations that persistently roam in my head on January nights, my nose in the journal pages of that indispensable nineteenth-century eccentric, Henry David Thoreau. If anyone can coax you out of doors, it is young Henry; and so it is with me this morning.

I RESIDE A LONG WAY from Thoreau's local Concord and Sudbury rivers, pleasant streams both. Yet, having lived for years above one of Maine's great waterways, I have come to appreciate his motives. Thoreau walked out each day to Walden Pond long before he built his cabin on its bank. He could not easily sit still, and was forever in the process of going, if only in thought. Similarly, young Henry was a habitué of the Concord well before he navigated it. Like him, I would see my river on most days, walk or otherwise go by it, perhaps eating lunch at some neighborhood counter that offered a view of the moving water. Looking downstream on many afternoons, I connected with the literal river and was drawn in. Rivers are things not easily resisted.

As my winter attentions went increasingly to regional maps and to histories on the shelves of the Maine State Library, some other data captured my interest. Any historically minded soul not in the grip of school-bookery will conclude that Maine is the earliest consistent link in European colonization of the New World. We were all instructed otherwise, of course, but, from the late 1400s, Maine became the landfall of explorers, would-be settlers, merchant companies, fishermen, and traders motivated to see what lay beyond the limiting ocean. Some evidence and much speculation suggest that they were preceded by itinerant Norsemen and, perhaps, even by hardy Irish explorers in leather boats. (As if to settle any doubts, not long ago, a band of Maine men made such a journey from east to west, from Scandinavia to landfall in Maine, in a wooden longboat exactly like those the Norsemen used.) From the earliest days of America, Maine was where travelers first came ashore.

These waterborne travelers scouted the Maine coast and turned upward into her beckoning rivers as if loudly summoned. Each successive wave of visitors, whatever their stated purpose, maneuvered boats up into the Kennebec, Sheepscot, Damariscotta, and their smaller sister rivers. Visitations did not stop once coastal settlements were founded, either. This push up Maine's great tidal rivers continued into the colonial and post-colonial years as ambitious men extracted a wealth of timber, fur, and fish. The settling of eastern America along these rivers and coves became a major factor in colonial unrest and in the new-minted nationhood that followed.

Along these same shores, Abenaki Indians of the Algonquin nation first welcomed the British and then fought with them, bruised by ill use. Later, they would contend with arriving Massachusetts Bay colonists who had come northeast to settle in the aboriginals' midst. Raids, skirmishes, and pitched battles alternated with periods of nervous calm. Filled with hearty contempt for the native, British traders cheated tribal peoples routinely, and a once cordial connection deteriorated. Eventually, marauding parties on both sides went up and down the rivers, each seeking the advantage of the other.

Upriver from where I live stretches the territory that fueled the greatest expansion of shipbuilding, shipping, and seaborne military might ever witnessed in preindustrial society. If the lower reaches of rivers hereabouts were once gates open to the world, upstream lay the raw resources, the millions of acres of timber that stood in cold valleys and on mountain ridges, destined to be felled to become ships. So much wood lay here for hulls and masts that the aristocracy of England, France, and the Low Countries thought of it and salivated, like hungry dogs in jealous anticipation of meat. Two centuries later, those same timber lots fed the rivers with pulpwood bound for the paper mills of the Northeast. For more than a century and a half, the Kennebec and its neighboring Sheepscot and Damariscotta rivers ferried either this woodsy commerce or other spoil onward to a waiting world.

Even exploitation relents. These rivers are quieter today, returning to something of their earliest selves. Still, with a little imagination, you can feel the weight of all this history, community building, downriver commerce, and the change that has followed. Here and there, the old pocket booms still dot the water. Swelling tides drift miles up from the Atlantic Ocean to the Kennebec's first dam at Waterville. Fishing remains an enduring element of river commerce on the Sheepscot and Damariscotta. The thread continues.

Up north, the great rapids of the Kennebec Gorge still thunder, host now to whitewater rafters instead of timber drivers. Similarly, the narrow headwaters of the Sheepscot plummet over rock falls in hidden little villages, and the Damariscotta, where I am making ready to set out this morning, catches the outflow of the lake and feeder streams above it. Farther along the coast, the St. George, the Pleasant, and the Machias drop through sleepy, remote settlements, some without so much as a general store. Everywhere there are reminders of the transforming power of rivers, effects forever incorporated into both the region's and the nation's history. There are memories here.

Living in the midst of all this, I wished for a deeper experience of these various waters, of what they have meant and of what they might mean today. A wish, I suppose, to exchange the distant view from land for the view from the water, from the surface of the river itself. Seat-of-the-pants research is not without merit. My winter's reacquaintance with Thoreau awakened old affections. His example, I concluded, was worthy of emulation. These rivers of Maine's midcoast had gradually become, for me, not merely something seen occasionally in passing, but a living entity that seemed so essential to my own sense of place and history that I arranged to draw closer. To improve my acquaintance with these old neighbors, I would experiment a bit with navigation.

The Kennebec, Sheepscot, and Damariscotta nestle comfortably close to one another, and shorter streams and backwaters connect them in interesting ways. I would have no absolute route in mind as I set out, other than making my way through the most attractive reaches of each, upriver or down, pausing to observe what dwells there. Travels where every moment is planned down to the last detail somehow defeat curiosity. I would be careful not to burden myself with anything resembling a schedule. My only commitment would be to roam and observe within the limits of seven or eight days.

My hoped-for river explorations would not be entirely casual and directionless, however. Like Thoreau, I wanted to improve upon a personal knowledge of the familiar. Such investigations begin, inevitably, near home. Thoreau and his brother set out on the Concord River in August of 1839 in a wooden dory they named *Musketaquid* and rowed into a network of streams and rivers that linked their own neighborhood with territory to the north. Thoreau enjoyed such journeys as a means of seeing how his at-home world joined to something larger. He was a man forever concerned with what could be learned about the complexities of place, and so, it seems, am I. Henry saw spiritual and intellectual forms in the physical river, shore, forest, and hill, and I like his way of looking at things. It was as little as I might do to follow his example.

My kind of intended exploration isn't in the least fashionable. It is more modern to prefer Pago Pago, of course. But elaborate journeys in honor of remote, overseas obscurities have always puzzled me. It's rather like saying that a countryside and its inhabitants are interesting only if they are far away, uncomfortably strange, and difficult to reach. In today's world, escape to far-away wildernesses may be illusory in any case. Fly to the ends of the earth, put your boat in the water, and you collide with crowds who have beaten you to it, waving frantically from noisy marinas. Or, perhaps a *National Geographic* film crew, breaking for lunch. What, precisely, is the purpose of being forever in search of elsewhere? In an era where we can fly to almost anyplace on the planet in a few hours, it is actually the texture of our own turf from which we have become disconnected, divorced. My sentiments go with those who choose to look geographically inward. On this week's journey I meant to get back in touch.

Leafing through old journals, I perused Ernest Marriner's *Kennebec Yesterdays,* Garnett Laidlaw Eskew's writing on Kennebec shipbuilding history, Robert P. Tristram Coffin's *Kennebec: Cradle of Americans,* and Bruce Bourque's twelve-thousand-year history of Maine's native peoples. As I read, a larger, more engaging picture began to emerge, illustrating a way of life that, perhaps, existed nowhere else.

It was time for a conceptual regrouping. Having planned at first to explore only the Kennebec, I willingly extended my view to include more territory. My planned river excursion would require broadening. At the center of a great coastal triangle, the Kennebec, the Sheepscot, and the Damariscotta feed the Atlantic with watery arms that reach well back into Maine's hinterland. They have the stuff of history in common, a shared memory if you will. Collectively they nurture a place where forest and coastal ways of life have converged and where the life of early America stubbornly dug in, held on, and is still holding on.

Each of these rivers, familiar to me in a way, forms the circulatory system of my everyday inland and coastal haunts. But, of course, I had been viewing them from the land. I wanted to see the region through different lenses and from as many angles as I could manage. No one of these rivers, I began to see, could be considered in isolation. Quite immodestly for a landlubber, I decided I would explore sections of them all.

IT IS BRIGHTER NOW, and I walk *Merlin* slowly along the shoreline, getting free of submerged rock and ledge and looking for downriver traffic. The Damariscotta continues quiet. I climb in and make snug the spray skirt, and with a few strokes align Merlin's narrow bow upriver and north. The sun has made a full appearance, but the wind holds off. I stow one paddle and hold the boat against the tide for a moment with the other, taking in the scent of the day and the river. When I have lingered long enough I turn into the current, the sky now promising, herring gulls circling my little craft, *Merlin* poised to move upriver. Like Thoreau, I have borrowed some time to see what I can see of the moving water to which I had grown attached. I mean to visit the upper navigable length of the Damariscotta, the top end of the Sheepscot to Head Tide, and the lower half of the Kennebec, if tides and hours allow. Perhaps I will go farther. I am determined to let nature and history guide these days. I set my paddle, *Merlin* turns to work, and we head north.

PHOTOGRAPH BY DIANNA RUST

Day One

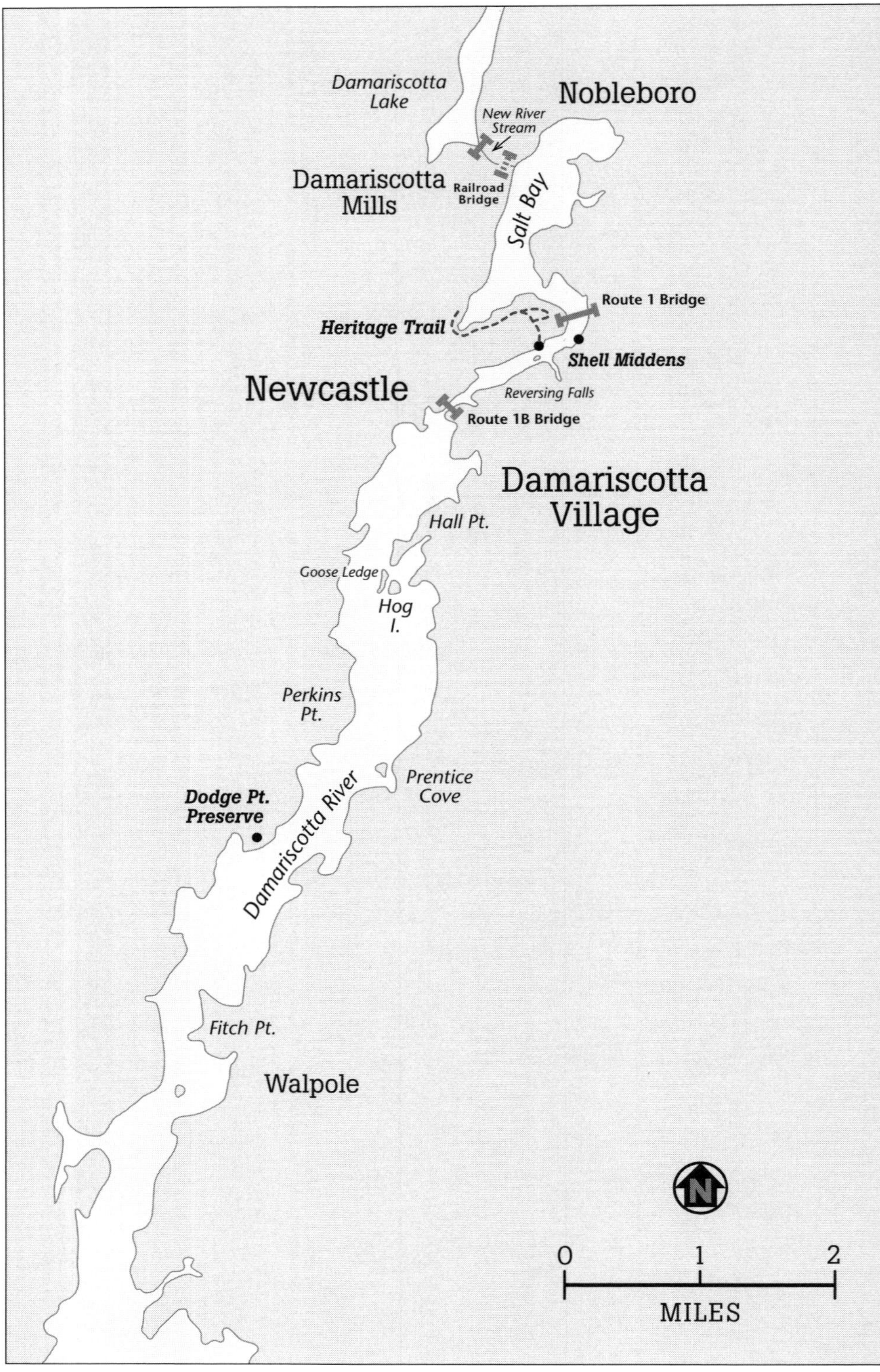

Damariscotta Lake
Nobleboro
New River Stream
Damariscotta Mills
Railroad Bridge
Salt Bay
Route 1 Bridge
Heritage Trail
Shell Middens
Newcastle
Reversing Falls
Route 1B Bridge
Damariscotta Village
Hall Pt.
Goose Ledge
Hog I.
Perkins Pt.
Prentice Cove
Dodge Pt. Preserve
Damariscotta River
Fitch Pt.
Walpole
N
0
1
2
MILES

The Damariscotta

It is the Middle Coast that is the heart of maritime Maine. This is the land of the great forested rivers. "A great river is equivalent," it is said, "to a great key unlocking the resources of a country." The middle coast has a ringful of these keys to the treasure chest that is central Maine.

William Hutchinson Rowe
The Maritime History of Maine (1948)

I pull to the left side of the broad river with Fitch Point downstream and at my back. Hugging the shore, I face Dodge Point upriver off my bow. Although I've walked the point's dense woods in numerous earlier seasons, I have never seen this large, beautiful state preserve from the water. On a sloping rise that ascends inland, a fine stand of cultivated red pines backed by mixed-growth forest crowns the point. A network of pretty trails wanders here, and you can laze about for hours in this quiet forest.

On my walks here I have seen bald eagles and ospreys perched in treetops from which these active birds launch fishing expeditions over the river. I get a particular satisfaction in seeing sections of river land like this protected from development. Purchased from the Edward Freeman Trust in 1989, the five-hundred-acre point was brought into the fold of state lands through the efforts of the Land for Maine's Future Program, the Maine Bureau of Public Lands, and the state planning office's Maine Coastal Program. Support for operation and maintenance of the preserve comes from the Damariscotta River Association. These various entities together have kept a precious bit of woodland in its natural state, preventing developers from reducing its exquisite terrain to sixty-five shoulder-to-shoulder house lots, as they once were bent on doing.

An old brick foundry once did its work here, close to the water. Maine clays are often very suitable for brick making. The foundry is now long disappeared, but one can occasionally find bricks protruding from the mud on what has been called Brickyard Beach. *Merlin* slowly coasts the shore as I look for errant remnants of the brickworks. Riding an early incoming tide extracts a cost, however. Even with *Merlin*'s shallow draft, I find I can't get close enough to shore to do a wander without a lengthy trek across embracing tidal mud. I decide to push on.

I quickly move north, the tide at my back. Prentiss Cove and its diminutive island lie across on the eastern shore. The river continues wide, but no longer vacant. Past Perkins Point, there is a continual surprise in the number and extent of aquaculture plantations in coves and inlets on both sides of the Damariscotta. Floating buoys mark submerged plots in the shoals. Men in boats tend the frames. I slow to watch them for a moment and rest the paddle. Elsewhere, tenders move about, repairing, harvesting. A friend, I remember, pioneered this form of river aquaculture along Maine's southern coast in the York River many years ago. I wonder if he and his family are still there. Diverse methods of fish and shellfish harvesting are practiced up and down this coast now, and each helps deliver a significant chunk of Maine's saltwater earnings. A man in a battered hat and waders hails, and I wave back in the quiet camaraderie of the river.

The Damariscotta is hospitable only to craft of moderate draft along these reaches. Charts show five to seven feet here and seventeen feet at middle channel, perhaps less as the tide diminishes. Staying nearer the western shore as I paddle, I occasionally strike bottom with the blade. This river has exerted its force by carving a path for itself sideways rather than digging particularly deep into resistant bedrock, a characteristic it shares with its sister rivers.

Geologists have remarked at how distinctive the land formations of the midcoast region actually are. A glance at a map shows numerous parallel river basins extending north and south, leading inward from the sea. Formerly submerged seabed was folded more than 400 million years ago here and then invaded by molten granitic plutons, especially on the southern coast. The folded land formed basins that became natural collection points for runoff, and the rivers were born. After the last ice age, ending roughly eleven thousand years ago, sea level rose and pushed salt water up and between these riven folds of bedrock, leaving Maine with this astonishing riverine coast.

I am relieved to find that the Damariscotta displays relatively little of the wall-to-wall cottage effect seen on many Maine waterfronts. I see a few scattered rooftops on the east shore as I stroke northward, but the motif is mainly one of dense hardwoods. The sounds of hammering and a tractor in a hidden field come across the water. A pair of great blue herons probe the shallows where the water runs cloudy. Hay mixed with kelp and bits of topsoil from lands well above here circles in eddies, flushed down through Damariscotta Lake and its entry to the river. I paddle my way through a medium of exchange.

The Damariscotta River was originally known by its Abenaki eponym, *Madameskontee,* or "place of many alewives." After initial settlement of New England by Europeans, a series of hostilities with Indians erupted, first in Massachusetts and then with tribes across the region, including Maine. The raids in this vicinity were a part of that series of continuing hot and cold regional conflicts known as King Philip's, King William's, Queen Anne's, and Lovewell's wars. Sporadic Indian hostilities drove settlers from river communities from 1675 onward. As soon as the raids ceased, enterprising settlers returned. Fishing and shipbuilding gained their ascendancy, along with brick making, boot making, tanning, and manufacture of matches.

Ahead, an island lies nearer the east shore. I make for it, skirting another aquaculture bed. Hog Island is a wooded, steeply banked mound that rises at a sharp angle from the water. *Merlin* snakes up a channel to the right, and then we turn northwestward as Hall Point comes into view. In the foreground, herring gulls and cormorants walk about raised, granite Goose Ledge, nattering and bleating at one another. Overhead, a great blue heron, its wings broadly expanded and legs extended back like ailerons, throttles downriver as if late for an appointment. Slowly, *Merlin* makes the circuit of the quiet cove and we emerge again in the larger river.

The Damariscotta River below Great Salt Bay

ALL OF THE RIVERS on my plate during this journey have an interesting geological underlayment, as I've noted. Before setting out, I was curious to know exactly what hid under the rivers I was navigating. Inspired by several summer evenings with geology books, I got a Bedrock Geological Map of Maine and tried to figure it out. A year of historical and physical geology studied in my undergraduate years (before the last ice age) was only of very modest help as I puzzled my way through this blanket-sized map spread out on a wide table.

This much I discovered: The mouths of the rivers I would travel are situated within a vast littoral known as the coastal lithotectonic block. At their mouths, they are underlaid by mélange deposits of Ordovician and Precambrian rock common to this block. Slightly inland, on the west side of the Norumbega Fault, they touch or cross into the Kearsage–Central Maine synclinorium. Maine's lower midcoast, where these rivers enter the sea is, then, a kind of separate shelf, with a major fault line not far inland.

The Kennebec rests on more of the Ordovician layer, now a sulfidic/carbonaceous pelite, as one traces its bed northward. It cruises next over a Silurian-Ordovician layer of basaltic intrusion as it continues inward, and then over alternating layers of lower and upper Silurian rock. The Damariscotta makes a shallower intrusion as it runs over calcareous Devonian and Ordovician stone after bridging the common coastal rocks. The Sheepscot fares similarly in the miles it covers below Head Tide. That these rocks are estimated to be at least four hundred million years old is staggering.

If one looks at a horizontal profile of these submerged layers, it is easy to see that the rivers intrude relatively little into the hidden rock. Still, from the map, I could see how each of the rivers I am traveling has invaded this ancient, layered coastline and made a bed for itself, the Kennebec's being the most exploratory. I would be seeing mainly shallow riverbeds all week, and the map, with its elaborate illustration of the variegated underlayment present here, provided clues to the shape of each river. As I will later confirm firsthand when navigating the falls above on the Damariscotta and then the Sheepscot, this hard bedrock has resisted millennia of moving water nibbling at its surface. When the substrate is as tough as that found here, moving water pushes sideways at the adjacent shores rather than down into the bedrock to excavate its channel.

These three rivers are broad in many places and getting more so. With limited exceptions, they have indeed added to capacity by chipping away laterally. In a few places, such as the Kennebec just below Fiddler Reach and in limited sections of the other rivers, the bottom lies deeper because resistant rock to each side has concentrated water flow and fostered burrowing over centuries. Just opposite Atkins Bay on the Kennebec, for example, there are spots more than seventy or eighty feet deep, and there are even deeper areas at the mouth of the Kennebec where especially strong currents have bored downward. It seems an even match; if the stone is immutable, water is relentless.

I HAVE BEEN on the water long enough this morning to begin to feel my stride, the paddle thrusting easily in its endless alternating plunge. Each stroke, really a push on the raised end of the shaft, is a search for efficiency. A certain pleasant mindlessness descends while I think of the history of this place, what it must have looked like to those who came upriver four hundred years ago, and what signs of their passing remain. As I trade stroke for stroke, the boat responds as if worn rather than steered, so comfortable and steady is the synchrony. Such is the virtue of the kayak.

Alternatively, sitting in a canoe, as some of us have done hundreds of times, can be rather like perching in a waterborne chair that makes a habit of turning on you as it plays in the current. I've been lucky enough over the years not to get wet in this manner. Still, I have periodically dried off companions who, after successfully completing a canoe trip in a state of dreamy serenity, embraced the dock, swung to shore, and plunged headfirst into the current. Tricky things, those.

A long tradition of canoe manufacture lives on in Maine. For many, especially in the rapids of the north, the canoe remains the watercraft of choice when one doesn't want to listen to the unpleasant clatter of motors all day. The choice, that is, until someone talks you into sallying forth in a kayak and trying out that equally ageless means of transport. I did that a number of years ago, and, because I had grown tired after twenty-plus years of inelegant J-stroking, found the kayak greatly to my liking. My canoe was advertised and sold. (I say all this as one who still loves canoes.)

An argument could be waged as to which is the older, more time-tested craft, though I think the kayak would win. The baidarkas of the Inuit and Aleut people are very old indeed. Kayaks certainly would triumph in matters of efficiency. There are exceptions, admittedly. Get two skilled canoe operatives in a fine old E.M. White or Chestnut, and chances are they will exact penance from a river or lake in short order, leaving those paddlers proud, if tired. On the other hand, canoes can be absolute dogs in crosscurrents and high winds, and paddling long distances alone can be a chore. I was reminded of this again on a recent windy canoe trip up the usually reticent Concord River along Thoreau's route of 1839. If you are covering water by yourself, as I am this morning, efficiency and a certain promptness are desirable, and *Merlin* offered just that in the way a solo canoe might not.

Merlin arrived in my back yard after a conversation I had with Joe Dryden at Eddyline on the West Coast. We had agreed that *Merlin*, at fifteen feet, sported the length-width proportions that favored adequate speed and the responsive maneuvering I required, with minimum weight. This week of river paddling is a kind of test run. *Merlin* represents the earliest of a new series of craft made from a material called Carbonlite 2000, a high-technology blend that is tough, superlight, and beautiful. Carbonlite is, as the name implies, easier to lift. In off hours, *Merlin*'s forty-six pounds lifts agreeably to the roof of my car. After the awful polyethylene tubs I have forced up rivers in an earlier life, *Merlin* shows signs of being the best of companions, sliding northward easily, gracefully. One falls in love immediately with things that are easy to lift.

I PADDLE NORTHWARD, keeping slightly to the right of midstream now. Beyond Hall Point, Damariscotta Village comes into view, draped like some painterly mural along the northern horizon. Damariscotta is an old place, as I have hinted. It has slowly grown in the embrace of the river. In the midst of my view, still at some distance, stands "the bridge," a present-day steel span that replaced the wooden arches that preceded it. The bridge has long been the central point of Damariscotta's local geography, and an interesting little neighborhood has grown around it.

Stroking steadily along, we pass a series of coves, some of which hosted shipbuilding firms during the post-colonial era. Damariscotta boomed as a place of ship construction in the early and mid-1800s. Across the river, in Newcastle, William Walters constructed ships of 400 tons burthen as early as 1772. Enoch Dole, Teague and Hall, Joseph Glidden, and Thomas Rowe turned out a continuous stream of brigs and schooners in the youthful days of the shipbuilders' trade on the western limits of this broad harbor.

If I crane my neck rightward I can see where the Day family dominated ship construction on the east side of the Damariscotta. Their output ranged from the brig *Goldhunter* in 1828 and the 1,500-ton *Lucy Thompson* in 1852, to the 1,350-ton *Voyager* in 1874, the latter fashioned by the combined yards of Day and Curtis. These craft and dozens of others would find their way into the West Indies trade initially, and then outward to the oceans of the world.

Getting finished ships downriver to the open sea was a separate matter, however. A certain conniving and chicanery was seen around these yards when a newly constructed ship was ready for the river. *The Lincoln County News* of January 29, 1920, recalled the story of one ship's progress from the Day yard unusually late in the season. Ships typically were lowered to the river in May, and post-launch fitting and rigging might go on for weeks, but, in 1857, delays kept the 1,183-ton *Success* in harbor until the autumn. Delay compounded delay. Ice, should you wonder, will quite efficiently imprison and crush the hull of a wooden ship, so the owners of the *Success* were anxious to get the ship to sea, where it would escape the ice and begin earning its keep. As the temperature dropped, the ship's captain negotiated for a tug to pull the large vessel downriver as soon as it was ready.

Still the ship tarried, and negotiations continued as ice began to form. The steam tug owner, seeing his advantage, took a measure of the weather and doubled his price with the advent of November cold. He hadn't correctly reckoned on the boldness of the *Success*'s captain, however. Rather than pay extortionate rates to get his ship to sea, the captain ordered all sails hoisted and tight reefed.

Wind filled the spread canvas, and the *Success*, its bowsprit faced downriver, groaned through the hardening ice, making its own way safely to the Atlantic. This was, I would guess, the first instance of the vessel justifying its name.

THERE ARE NO ships of *Success*'s girth in harbor as I arrive at Damariscotta this morning, but more modern sail craft linger, some at anchor, one or two lazily raising sail for the downriver jaunt. I navigate the east side of the harbor pool and put in to shore at the town ramp. Englishman John Brown arrived similarly at what was then known as New Harbor, Pemaquid, sometime before 1625. Brown soon purchased land from two Penobscot sagamores, according to deeds that date from that year. He built a house near the site of the Damariscotta bridge, just a stone's throw from here on the river's east bank by the falls. Members of the Brown family intermarried with the Alexander Goulds, of Bremen, and the Richard Pearce family, of Muscongus, and the early signs of a regional dynasty were in place. Brown expanded his holdings until they covered a good deal of what is now Bristol, Bremen, Damariscotta, Nobleboro, and some of Newcastle, Jefferson, and Waldoboro. All of this area became known as New Dartmouth, or simply Dartmouth, after its settlers' English origins.

I walk around the town briefly, temporarily giving up the wet world of the river for the bustle of Damariscotta's Main Street. Procuring a bite to eat at a local counter, I compare the old, battered pickup trucks with newly arrived Mercedes, BMWs, and Saabs that compete for parking space in the town lot. Here is a lesson in sociology often repeated during the Maine summer. After the decline of its shipbuilding days, Damariscotta lay for years as a sleepy little river village until discovered as, first, a good town near which to have a summer cottage, and, later, a retirement community for the financially comfortable from elsewhere. Plain folks' stores for those of my wealth, such as Renys, still exist here, but upscale *shoppes* have spread up Main Street as if stridently on the march. On the Fourth of July, the village still acquits itself with a rather commendable fireworks display, rockets shooting out over the harbor where I will next maneuver farther northward.

Once again at the landing, I board and make an arc around a tangle of moorings, getting back into the current. The river exerts itself more powerfully now. In the narrow funnel of the bridge, where the entire contents of the harbor spill upstream through a fifty-foot opening, I feel an energetic kick from the incoming tide. Passing under the bridge and into another world, I ride over submerged falls that create whitewater here at low tide. A few large, old houses peek through the trees.

When a rapidly moving tidal river is forced into a new channel less than one-fifth its previous size, interesting things happen. All those forces that spread across the wider bay downstream have to work themselves along a narrower, ledgy bottom here. As I had anticipated, the submerged bedrock in this section of the river shows little sign of relenting. Several resistant bands of rock create a navigational hazard here at low water. I must watch the clock or I will find myself aground on ledge on my return. On the river's surface, great whorls of troubled water compete with crosscurrent lines and eddies. Tame enough at certain hours, the river now requires more attention, the current quite willing to push *Merlin* toward some undesired compass point. Like some aging wines, the Damariscotta alters its flavor here, becoming a bolder, more capricious river.

The current gallops along the western shore, its progress visible on the water's surface as the stream gradually widens. The river tries to grab *Merlin*'s stern and force us toward one shore or the other, like being grabbed by the shoulders from behind and twisted first left and then right. As we drift more to the right, the tidal shove eases a bit. Ahead, the river pulls steadily around to the northeast. The shore offers fewer signs of civilization, and to the north I see a small island and the telltale signs of whitewater. Not far beyond are a second and third set of ledges demanding my attention. One lies off the west end of this little island, the other a few hundred yards beyond. I have not reconnoitered this stretch of river before, and the guidebooks suggest that sobriety and an attitude of respect are appropriate. I put some muscle into my stroke and climb toward the tidal rapids ahead.

Two channels appear. I can stay with the main river to the left and take whatever the ledges in front of me provide, or choose a second channel that

Boat landing, Damariscotta River

skirts the island to the right. I explore this second alternative, but it looks rough and not promising. The drop appears abrupt; water races through the narrow channel, and rocks and points of ledge stand like picket fences in that direction. I paddle hard against the current, slowly working my way around the island to the west. Here the main channel races over the ledges, which by no means are well covered yet, making for a risky passage that threatens possible grounding and overturn. I find a narrow sluice between the island and the most prominent section of ledge and let the tide push me into it.

There proves to be enough depth and movement here, and I rocket through, finding myself coasting upstream beyond the second ledge. Looking around, I am surprised to find a line of canoes occupied by nervous kids from a nearby camp sheltering in the lee of the island. An attractive camp counselor waves to me, and I wave back, eager to convince her that I am, indeed, a bold man of the rapids. Her charges wait anxiously for a lesson in holding a canoe steady in a galloping current. Another counselor takes each canoe, one at a time, out into the rolling current, and I watch to see how the occupants do and, perhaps, learn a few things. There are no capsizes, but I witness a lot of frantic, desperate paddling to hold the boats against the swift current.

As much as I want to backtrack and discuss matters of northern exploration with my newfound waving acquaintance, it is clear that the river will not wait. It hurries onward and I move with it, searching for a place to aim *Merlin* as we approach still another bank of rough water. A large stone formation juts out from the eastern shore past mid-river; certainly, there is no passage in that direction. Several cormorants sun themselves on a mid-river rock. I wish they could share their knowledge as to where the deepest water might be found. Ferrying closer to the west side of the river, I push into the main current again. This is not a place where one can dally musing on the state of the world—I must do *something*. Aligning *Merlin*'s bow with the main path of the surging current, I roll through, crossing the rock bar. There is depth enough, but not much more; I see ledge flash by beneath me as I shoot ahead. The cormorants nod.

I PADDLE TO THE NORTHEAST, the river edge a series of little gravel beaches and brilliant green marsh to my left. Somewhere not far along the increasingly high right bank is an Indian site I want to visit, and I scan the shore for the tiny landing spot where *Merlin* might rest. A muddy stretch of banking bearing the imprint of several canoe bows seems to be the place, and I haul ashore. Above, the faint line of a path leads to a great Abenaki shell midden, an ancient depository of Indian shells or, less elegantly, a very large, old Native American dump. I am not usually enthused about frequenting dumps, but this one defies comparison. It contains hundreds of thousands of shells left here by tribes who fled to the coast in summer to fish and escape the depredation of insects in the northern woods. They obviously feasted well, as their leavings are strikingly ample. Across the river lies a second midden.

This massive heap of detritus, now surmounted by shrubs and trees, is evidence of a society that intelligently managed its year and reaped the benefits of both inland hunting and coastal harvesting. It is an odd reminder of transience. I try to envision what it must have been like to camp hereabouts, to fish and to harvest shellfish, to gather berries and to do the summer work that would make survival possible in the Maine winter to follow. These people were intimately bound up with the labors of their existence, work that formed the adhesive of community, rather than the alienating separateness of this existence we call modern. I would as lief picnic with them, I think.

The shell heaps, estimated to be more than two thousand years old, also might be viewed as a testament to the careful use of a resource. The stable and productive native cultures of the Northeast embraced a make-do frugality that included an attitude of conservation. Shellfish aside, animals taken in hunting along these rivers often were eaten ceremoniously in their entirety. Waste of captured game was disrespectful of the animal that had offered its life, and nowhere was this truer than in killing bear. A black bear—powerful, remote, and mysterious—when flensed, reveals a skeleton surprisingly like that of a human. Its spirit may be immortal. Bear dances, with tribal members dressed in bearskins, could summon the sick and dying to health. The bear possessed so powerful a magic that it could not be mentioned directly, but was referred to as "young brother" or "old brother" in conversation.

This reverent husbanding of resources shows up frequently in native stories from the Northeast and eastern Canada. Legends have conveyed lessons, sometimes metaphorically, of what happens when humans are wasteful in the taking of animals. An old Micmac story shared by several tribes of the Northeast in various narrations recounts the tale of a wasteful killer and an animal rescue in deep history:

A tribal woman pregnant with twins is killed and eaten by a monster that comes to their camp. The monster rips the babies from her, but by then he has a full belly, so he leaves one twin behind and takes the other with him to eat later. The twin left behind is rescued and reared by the tribe. His brother is not eaten by the monster, but wastefully thrown away. This brother is rescued by animals, who rear him and make him healthy. He returns to the tribe and is reunited with his brother.

The twin brothers are now strong. They leave their camp to hunt for the monster and avenge their mother's death. They find the monster and slay it.

There is a nice logic to the story. When you are in danger and abandoned, animals—with whom you share kinship—may rescue you. They thus deserve your respect. Also, he who takes life and then wastes it will pay a penalty, as does the monster. For tribes who knew that a single bad season could be their undoing, waste was no less than monstrous.

The Smithsonian Institution has on display a drawing on birch bark made by Sapiel Selmo, a Passamaquoddy, depicting the legend of a hunter who made winter camp along a river, possibly the Penobscot or Machias. The story it tells goes like this:

The hunter searches. He hunts a bear and follows its tracks in the snow to where the bear is asleep in its den. The hunter is impatient and does not ask the bear's forgiveness before taking its life. He does not practice right spirit with this bear—he jumps in the den and stabs it. But his impatience defeats him. He has not stabbed the bear in the heart. The bear is only wounded, and it attacks him. The wounded hunter struggles homeward while the bear dies. The man scratches a map of the route to the bear den on a piece of birch bark and then dies, too. Using the map, the hunter's brothers return to the den and carry the bear to their camp. Now they show proper respect for this bear. They give him tobacco and thank him for giving himself. They make peace with this bear, and all is right.

THE RIVER MAKES its final jog to the northeast, passes a sand beach to the west, and runs under U.S. Route 1. The current divides here, forming three threads around the pilings of the bridge. As we sail over submerged ledge beneath the overpass, *Merlin* drops suddenly into an upstream trough as if sliding off a shelf. A return current coming down the west side of the bay slices across the entering tidal flow and applies some sideways pressure to *Merlin*'s stern. Recovering, I paddle hard up the little bay to the northwest.

My progress here is through the entry to Great Salt Bay, a broad, shallow, windswept catchment that collects the outflow of Damariscotta Lake and the inland streams that feed it. The bay is undergoing a kind of renaissance, its shores now host to a hiking trail and a restored alewife ladder connecting the bay with the lake above. Shellfish farming occurs here, too, and I paddle through scattered floats and grids. As I move more northwesterly toward the larger impoundment, the current ceases to be a factor, but the wind, steady and gusty out of the north, pushes at *Merlin*'s bow. We take shelter behind a small neck of land, and for a brief moment things are quiet. A strategy meeting is in order.

I debate whether to cross the bay along its southern shore or keep to an ascent up its east side. I eventually want to reach the bay's northwest corner and its connector with Damariscotta Lake. Given the wind's direction, I am going to be lambasted either way, so I set my course toward the northwest and enter the open bay with the intent of testing the strength of the wind. There has been a wind all day, but in the sheltered course of the river, with dense foliage and high ground on both sides of the channel, the impact has been minor. No longer. I paddle the shallows, staying east of a tiny island in mid-bay, the gusts of wind making me work for every inch I gain. I explore eastward into a small inlet and see, on a distant rise, a white farmhouse above pasture, the headquarters of the Damariscotta River Association.

The late poet and author Elizabeth Coatsworth, for years lived just up the road from here with her husband, writer and naturalist Henry Beston. In one of her books she retold the local story of a witch who lived along the Damariscotta. The old woman was said to have made her living by selling wind. One day the witch overheard two captains boasting of the speed of their ships as they waited to begin a run to Boston on the morrow. One of these captains was from this region, and the witch favored him. Secretly urging him to bet all he had on winning the race to town and to leave that night under cover of darkness, the hag promised to keep his sails filled if he did as she said.

As instructed, the Damariscotta captain sailed in the night, and with a stiff wind pushing his ship along for the duration, he and his crew made record time to Boston. They had loaded a new cargo aboard and were ready to return to Damariscotta by the time his astonished competitor arrived. The Damariscotta captain also collected a sizable bag of gold on his wager. That witch surely is at work today, but not on *my* payroll, and she seems determined to make my upstream progress harder.

Moving slowly, I push into the wind again, heading northwest to the top of the bay, with *Merlin* shedding water over his streamlined bow. A handful of traditional houses line the shore at Nobleboro, their dark shutters and brilliant white clapboards striking a typical New England note. Bald eagles were fishing here in earlier weeks. The wind now asserts itself to the point where I have to accelerate my stroke merely to make headway; another ten or fifteen minutes of this, and we are at last in the lee of the bay's west bank. Paddling under a railway bridge, I emerge in a small, protected cove leading to a fish ladder here in the Damariscotta Mills section of Nobleboro. I nudge *Merlin* to shore to rest a while.

This fish ladder, which dates to 1807, connects Salt Bay with Damariscotta Lake via New River Stream. It was the work of John Perkins and Ephraim Rollins, who created a series of resting pools and sluices to form a navigable path for anadromous alewives *(Alosa pseudoharengus)* swimming upstream to spawn. The alewife harvest became an important seasonal industry, and as many as eighteen thousand bushels were taken in a single season. The catch gradually shrunk, however, and the towns of Newcastle and Nobleboro established a moratorium on fishing in hopes of boosting the numbers of fish moving upstream.

In recent years, with support from author and naturalist John Hay, local volunteers restored the partially fractured ladder, which transports migrating fish over a forty-two-foot rise. Stonemason Charles Hyson led the re-laying of stonework that ice and currents had pushed awry over the decades. The fish come running usually at the end of the first week in May, their movement a dense, silvery stream of activity. The migrating alewife and its free passage here is, in a way, one of the many hallmarks of the health of marine life on the coast.

The alewives are not running today; their season is yet months before me. Turning *Merlin*, I begin my descent of the west side of Great Salt Bay. The wind is less of a nuisance now, and it gradually lends itself to helping me southward. It has not lost its power, and continues to thrust acres of whitecaps toward the southeast. Stroking steadily, I again pass the island, a small rise in the bay's midst, brush-covered and supporting a few wind-bent trees. I spot no other craft on the water. In half an hour, the downwind scoot delivers me to the southwesternmost tip of the bay and the onshore trailhead for the new Salt Bay Preserve Heritage Trail.

Although there are cars parked by the trail board, I see no one about on this breezy afternoon. Hikers depart here for a three-mile stroll along the southern periphery of the bay, rounding Grandfather, Picnic, and Lookout points. Bald eagles and ospreys fish the shallows and a variety of other avian wildlife nests in the forest and marsh nearby. The trail turns southwest and explores an impounded tidal salt marsh and, later, the shores of a small pond before returning to the road. I make a mental note to walk it someday soon.

HAVING MADE the circuit of the bay, I now face the small matter of the return run to Damariscotta Village. I rode up on the tide, but I don't want to wait too much longer to head back downriver, for fear of being stranded. Many points in this shallow bay are above water at low tide. On the other hand, if I start downstream before slack tide, I will encounter water that is still moving briskly inward. Having already fought the bay winds, I have no yen to work harder than necessary on the return trip. The breeze rips at *Merlin*'s deck rigging as I drift a while to feel what the current is doing.

Impatience eventually gets the better of me. Paralleling the Heritage Trail alongshore, I work my way northeast and east toward the junction of bay and river under the U.S. Route 1 bridge. What I find is not comforting. Though by this hour the tidal inrush must have slowed well south of here, the river is still transporting tons of water northward, and I have to paddle strenuously to reach the channel's east side. Ferrying across the main thread of current beneath this high bridge amounts to real work, with more to come. *Merlin* begins to drift broadside, north rather than south; falling back, I come at the inrush from another angle, paddling like there's no tomorrow.

The current slackens a little along the east shore, and I stroke southward. The camp canoe group has gone ashore on the river's west bank at one of the tiny sandy beaches. Some of the campers look quite wet. They are waiting for the tide, too. As they depart to explore the great shell mounds I visited earlier, I pull to the shore, halting a tad longer for the tidal bore to ease. The beautiful camp counselor waves one last time, and I dream of a desert island where she and I might seriously discuss logical positivism.

Bright sun on this narrow shelf feels welcoming, and it is a pleasant relief to be out of the sharp wind. I break out a late lunch and reflect on my excursion. The Damariscotta ranks as a beautiful waterway by any measure. It is not merely a conventional beauty, though there is that as well. Its complexion changes with each mile, and the rangy bay that crowns its navigable upper reaches adds to its appeal. It captures interest by being its natural self, a working river, and by remaining a place relatively free of destructive development—a river whose history rests easy and largely unsullied. I imagine how it would be to head up and across the bay on a quieter day with the surface like glass. There are such times, if you choose your day carefully, and perhaps I will paddle here again. For now, I sense myself drifting into lassitude, and then realize that I need to tackle the southward journey because a friend with a roof rack is meeting me back in Damariscotta Village.

Merlin works down the map as we make our way along the east shore and into several quiet coves. The wind, considerably diminished, floats downward over the treetops as I approach the upper ledges, now deeply submerged, and we sail smoothly above the rocks that had formed such a resistant barrier on the ascent. I wonder how tribal groups native to the area contended with the current here in their light bark canoes. Preparing to test my own muscle, I paddle within reach of the small island I passed earlier, exploring the narrow passage to its left. I would prefer to exit southward without having to contend with the track of main current, which flows to the northwest of the island, but I find that the tidal push is still at full spate in the southerly channel, and it is difficult to judge the location of submerged boulders. Even assuming I can make headway against the current in this narrow passage, the matter of holing *Merlin*'s skin on a sharp outcrop of ledge threatens. Reluctantly, I paddle to the other side of the island again and try the main current. For a brief, quiet moment, I stroke around the island's upstream side and reflect on the duration of tides. Technically, the clock is well past high tide, but this far upriver the enormous volumes of water pushed inward continue to move toward Great Salt Bay even though the flow has begun to ebb miles away, at the Damariscotta's mouth. Despite my dalliance and my attempts to time my outward trip, the stiff, incoming movement of water still thwarts me.

I make my way into the main channel, and feel the full force of the river again, with *Merlin* sinking his teeth into the current as I paddle south over the submerged ledges. The buried rock thrusts the flowing water upward in a standing wave. I steer slightly to the left and find that paddling rapidly will just about hold the boat in position, but will not allow me to proceed any farther. Again, I have a moment to reflect on my poor timing as I attempt to ferry leftward, closer to the island. I do not want the current to push me backward out of this chute. Here the current is marginally less forceful, and with very rapid stroking more reminiscent of driving a play boat in whitewater, I get past the rapids and into calmer water.

My sentiments run to a leisurely drift toward the village, but the current, though less energetic now, still requires further persistence with the paddle. I descend a line twenty feet out from the Damariscotta's east shore and poke into coves and outlets as I make my way toward the village. The river's alternate widening and narrowing yields to a diminishing channel that pulls to the southwest and south. Paddling steadily, I see the shape of the bridge in Damariscotta once again in the distance. The current still thrusts inward with enough force to make me attentive to the ledges I crossed earlier when headed upstream, and to the way the current now works around the bridge supports.

I end my travel for today at the town landing. *Merlin* has completed a leisurely ten miles without complaint. There have been no mutinies. Except for wind over the bay, the clear weather held well, and the river has provided a number of engaging turns, revealing itself modestly in its currents, bends, and ledgy bottom. With the wind down, the warmth of the late summer afternoon reasserts itself. Cars full of seasonal tourists pass to and fro across the span ahead, each a little capsule with windows rolled up and air conditioning on, occupants staring straight ahead, insulated from the sounds, sights, and smells of the river, the bay, the distant natural world.

Day Two

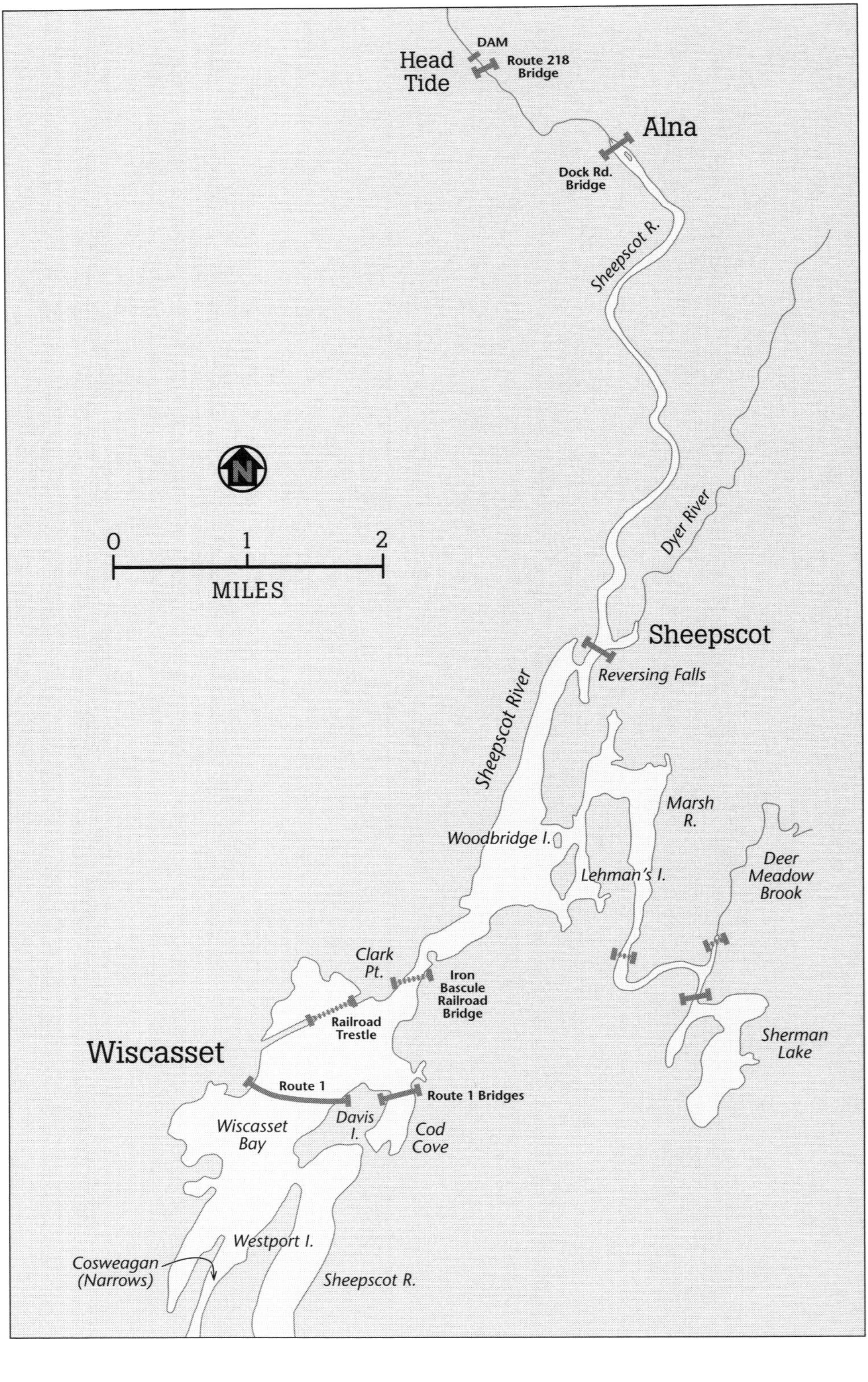
DAM
Head Tide
Route 218 Bridge
Alna
Dock Rd. Bridge
Sheepscot R.
Dyer River
0
1
2
MILES
Sheepscot
Reversing Falls
Sheepscot River
Marsh R.
Woodbridge I.
Lehman's I.
Deer Meadow Brook
Clark Pt.
Iron Bascule Railroad Bridge
Railroad Trestle
Wiscasset
Sherman Lake
Route 1
Route 1 Bridges
Wiscasset Bay
Davis I.
Cod Cove
Westport I.
Cosweagan (Narrows)
Sheepscot R.

The Sheepscot to Head Tide

About nine we got under way with a gentle breeze from the south-west, and fell down between Parker's Island and Jeremisquam into the Sheepscot river. The country hereabouts made a romantic appearance, fine groves of tall trees, shrubby evergreens, craggy rocks, cultivated fields and human habitation, alternately presented themselves to view, and yielded a profusion of pleasure to the imagination.

—Parson Jacob Bailey (1853)

I wash *Merlin's* decks, clearing away the river scum and bits and pieces of things picked up in the current, including twigs, tiny pieces of bark, the occasional leaf, and bits of straw mown in fields to the north. Even in a "clean" river, worlds of things float downstream, especially when farms along the water are mowing. Mid-morning has established itself, and I have a new river to travel. Securing *Merlin* on the roof of the car, I head for Wiscasset, a place often referred to by travel scriveners as "Maine's prettiest village."

Ideas about what constitutes pretty vary, of course, and, indeed, Wiscasset, a comely place of old Federal-style buildings and leafy side streets, pleases the eye. I tend to define pulchritude with a little more of an edge. Wiscasset still has a tiny working waterfront where fish and lobster are landed daily in the warmer months. That waterfront nicely rests at a point where the Sheepscot River widens to reassemble itself as a broad and inviting bay. Above the docks the old Customs House still stands, its graceful brick architecture a reminder of those days when shipbuilding and import-export wealth came tacking up or down the Sheepscot or arrived and departed via the two rail lines that served this dignified and prosperous village. This waterfront is my favorite corner of the town.

Wiscasset's downtown drapes itself over a hillside rising westward from the Sheepscot. As so often happened in New England towns, wealth arranged itself on the hillside according to degree and influence, so that one walks among modest streets with pleasant, small houses by the river and ascends to expansive mansions and churches at the crest, suggesting that God and mammon require a view. The courthouse is here, too, an old thing—in fact, one of the oldest courthouses anywhere in the United States. It still dispenses justice, but the building will soon be replaced. Its partner, the old jail, maintains its cold and hoary-headed presence on a hill north of the village center. The old jail no longer houses prisoners, but you may tour its chilly granite premises in summer for a couple of dollars and wonder at the ministrations of early American penology. In the days of conflict between liberty men and the great proprietors who had acquired parts of Maine after the Revolution, bands of angry settlers dressed in Indian garb raided the jail on several occasions, freeing those who had been arrested for refusing to pay unfair prices for the acreage they tilled.

Wiscasset, like Damariscotta, prospered as a shipbuilding locality. It competed with those very old shipbuilding sites I had passed on my climb up the Damariscotta and superseded them. In its early days, wooden vessels sprang from the ways at Wiscasset more often than any other American port until eventually that honor passed down the coast to Bath. The town acted as a transfer point for crops, fur, timber, and anything else marketable. Trade moved up and down the river and then to sea. At one time, the Maine Central Railroad and the Wiscasset, Waterville and Farmington Railway met here, the latter a two-foot narrow-gauge line that meandered up the backcountry through tiny villages and hamlets. One can still trace its roadbed through nests of brush in the woods.

The progress and wealth of Wiscasset's grandees led to a certain hubris. The local corporators of the narrow-gauge line originally planned to call their little railroad the Wiscasset and Quebec. What better aim, after all, than to connect the fine seaport of Wiscasset with the great cities of the St. Lawrence? In the end, the company managed to lay only forty-four miles of useful track, reaching from the harbor to the village of Albion upcountry. Cargo from inland not coming downriver by boat made the journey by two-foot gauge; it was then transferred to Maine Central cars at the substantial waterside yards of Wiscasset. Other goods made the leap to or from ships riding the Sheepscot here, bringing the world to Maine, and Maine outward to the world. The smaller railroad faded into eternity in 1933, but it is now being restored by a doughty team of volunteers as a kind of rolling museum.

I COULD SPEND a pleasant half-day walking about Wiscasset Village enjoying its hillside avenues, but I have a boat to launch. At the busy town wharf, I lower the kayak into the salty tide, organize the odds and ends I will carry upriver, and slip aboard. A woman and her daughter are paddling about the wharves in a leisurely way, and we compare weather notes. Out in midstream the tide runs slowly northward.

I like the look of Wiscasset Harbor. A resting place both for yachtsmen and fishermen today, the Wiscasset broads serve as home to a mixed flotilla of high-end sailing craft and Novi boats, Eastporters, and other working craft, nearly all of which disappear in winter. It's a democratic kind of harbor, and wears well for that.

This harbor is tied up in history. Somewhere on the opposite shore and downstream in Edgecomb, stood a house meant for Marie Antoinette—or at least so river storytellers have it. Believe what you will. Those who spin yarns say that Stephan Clough, an Edgecomb sea captain engaged in the French trade, was involved in plans to rescue Marie Anoinette and bring her to a house on this river. His ship, the *Sally*, had been secretly loaded with a substantial number of the lady's possessions and lay at anchor in a French harbor, ready to carry her safely to America. The currents of history ran in a different direction, however, and Marie Antoinette was carried to the guillotine in a tumbril rather than to the security of Clough's ship. The good captain quietly hoisted anchor and sailed home to Wiscasset with the unclaimed impedimenta of a queen in his hold. Local lore has it that these artifacts were kept in storage and eventually auctioned off. One Maine writer has suggested that items of Marie Antoinette's household, purchased at auction, can still be found, now and again, in Maine homes up and down the coast, symbols of the tumult of another era.

I paddle through the moorings and turn north along the west side of the bay, passing a big lobster car where herring gulls perch, eyeing me quizzically. My plan is to follow this northwest side of Wiscasset Bay where a little-used railroad trestle divides the bay from rafts of shallow flats. From there I will stay with the west shore, shortly passing under a great, arched railway bridge now as much the color of rust as its original black.

Paddling out into the channel, I clear the moorings and docks. The Sheepscot moves powerfully here, and inattention to tides at certain hours will send even a strong kayaker downstream toward the narrows despite rapid exercise of the paddle. As on the Damariscotta, I expect to ride upstream with the last hour or two of incoming tide, shamelessly cheating once again. Timing is essential. I need the inward flow of high water to get over the reversing falls that lie upstream in Sheepscot Village. The rising tide will carry me north through the shallows of the upper river to Head Tide village, the Sheepscot's navigable limit. Below me, the river departs from the bay, its main channel running around Westport Island, while the other drops via the chancy Narrows into Montsweag and Hockamock bays and then into a nest of tidal streams. I will come back later in the week to explore those waters on my last day out.

For now, my journey is to lead inward and beyond to what was once the heart of Sheepscot, if one dares say that Sheepscot had a precise center. A tangle of regional and royal grants, ancient Sheepscot was a subjective place, a rangy, ill-defined collection of settlements, fishing colonies, mill sites, Indian lands, and primitive hundred-acre farmsteads. It congealed around a number of useful natural anchorages up and down the river, the most prominent of which became Wiscasset.

Sheepscot and the grants that formed it were legacies of coastal settlement in the Pemaquid region and of the push of inland settlement that followed. Sometimes called Aponey, the community I'm headed for lodged itself between two courses of river above Wiscasset Bay. Sheepscot's connection with

Looking north from Sheepscot Village

the waiting sea made it a natural place to build, to transform, however slowly. Gazing upriver here in the early 1600s, one traveler enthused, "Taken all in all, a magnificent and profitable stream." Profitable it may have been, given the river's broad reaches—where large ships could be berthed, rigged, and turned—and, later, Wiscasset's ability to convert lumber to seaworthy ships of substantial tonnage. The Sheepscot itself was like a funnel: up the river went survival wares from England and down came a meager produce that would falter, disappear, and later slowly grow again. It would take time before prosperity gained hold. Looking upstream today leaves little doubt about the river's grandness. It has lost none of that.

I push *Merlin* along briskly, and we pass under U.S. Route 1, steering west of a raft of jagged, cormorant-occupied ledge that thrusts its head up through the current. I make a mental note of the location, as these sharp points might lie just under the surface later in the day. We keep close to the bay's west shore and inch along, making steady progress northward. A fine view of the old Wiscasset skyline rises over my left shoulder, a pleasant hodge-podge of bell towers, steeples, rooftops, and discordant gables. Along the waterfront, the wrecks of the *Hesper* and the *Luther Little* are now gone, the old schooner hulks broken up, carried away, freed forever from the lick of salt and mud. Somehow, I miss them.

I gain on the bay, its broad expanse capturing reflections of a brilliant sun behind me to the south. A small, densely wooded island lies to the right between me and expansive Cod Cove. Gulls perch in high, dead limbs, periodically launching themselves to dive for food. To the west, the railroad line crosses a long trestle. A breeze rolls down the hill behind it, passes through the trestle's pilings, and settles on the water. The air moves as the sun climbs, but with nothing like the force I encountered on Great Salt Bay yesterday. I am grateful for the relative calm; a wind from the northwest here can be daunting even in summer. All of Maine's great coastal rivers, with their north-south orientation, become funnels carrying northern winds downstream at full tilt and ocean-cooled air upstream in summer. If one knows the secrets of local geography, it is possible to sit oneself down on a spit of land along these rivers or adjoining bays on the hottest of July days and find cool contentment. Standing on the wharf from which I just launched can freeze your socks off on a windy January day if you are unprepared.

The west shore, pretty, wooded, and laced at its front with riverside shingle, leads me past Clark's Point to the railway bridge, a rusty, high, cantilevered span on which sit several large osprey nests, each looking like a giant twig farm. Ospreys possess a highly sensitive distant early-warning system in the form of astonishing vision. The adults take to the air and utter a chorus of scolding cries as I approach and paddle beneath the span. I stay distant enough that they refrain from further chatter. The incoming tide is compressed here as the bay becomes a river again at this bridge, and its current is deflected first left and then right. As the ospreys look down from overhead, I align *Merlin* and shoot through, pulling into the relative quiet of an eddy to the left. An adult osprey on top of the girders above is feeding at least one nestling. Another adult protects a second nest, while still another soars above, full of disapproval. Eventually deciding that I pose no threat, the large birds turn to things that are more important, and I resume paddling, pleased to have observed for a moment their domestic arrangements.

The Sheepscot, charged now with a whole bay full of advancing tide, moves along in a series of fluid skeins, lines of rapid, powerful current, each its own watery groove. Here the current boils, retreats, fights with itself, and tumbles uphill as the river maintains its narrowed course for a bit and then turns, widening out considerably. High ledges hidden in spruce and hemlock form a wall to the west as I make the turn through the confused strands of current and out into the gradually widening river.

WHAT IMPRESSES ME is that the Sheepscot, like the Damariscotta, is a quiet thread, nearly devoid of any boat traffic and with nearly no shoreline development. Other than the small cluster of fishing boats in the harbor at Wiscasset, the river doesn't seem to be heavily worked. Rarely, a lone workboat—usually a beamy, motorized dory skiff—passes, headed south, but then the river is quiet and empty again. I continue up the middle of the current, noting a house or two appearing on the west shore, sheltered back in the woods. This place must have seemed a paradise to those who arrived in the early 1600s, a place fecund, undisturbed, rich with promise.

What were they doing here, making their way up this river much as I am, pushing themselves forward in heavy boats around river bends and across water that no white-skinned people had seen before? What could bring these men, their imperiled families, their resilient women, up the Sheepscot's reaches into an unknown and perhaps lethal Eden, their hardy selves being their only tangible resource?

Were they tumbling up the strong currents of the river merely to increase their wealth, or the wealth of some proprietary grandee? If so, the odds of enterprise offered little reassurance. Did they see themselves as sloughing off England's religious or political restraints to establish a more egalitarian universe on these riverbanks? Or, were they set on farming land they actually might come to own rather than suffering brutal rack rents at home? Had they a conscious outcome in mind that justified the risk of one's scalp in woods and fields full of stealthy aboriginals who resented one's intrusion?

There had to be something more, after all, something that made the harrowing three-thousand-mile crossing in small ships endurable. Something that justified propelling oneself into an unforgiving, uncharted, unwelcome place where nothing existed save what one constructed with one's own hands and ingenuity.

More likely, some peculiar sense of destiny called them here. I do not mean the silly braggadocio of which Frederick Jackson Turner would later write—the white man's hubris driving him westward, the Europeans' thirst for possession urging migrants ever onward in some euphoria of heaven-ordained manifest destiny. I think the Sheepscot settlers saw a different, personal destiny waiting here for themselves and their kin. Perhaps a venue with a new set of rules, something unspoiled and thus simple, land not beset and held by ancient privilege. An opportunity to take the full measure of oneself in an utterly wild corner of the New World. The appeal is obvious, looking back from a modern century where too little that is new and unspoiled remains, and where Sherpas carry New York socialites on their backs to the highest summits of the Himalayas. The Sheepscot was a river and a shore of new beginnings, and its would-be occupants must have felt that promise as they came up this riverway perched on the very edge of the known world.

A COUPLE OF small boats swing at moorings and parts of a house become visible through the trees. On the east shore, a one-car-way freight rattles along the railroad line high on a bluff. Its sound bounces around the low pocket of the stream and then disappears south in a cut as the train heads for the bridge. I wonder what the ospreys will do with the noisy freight careening along just inches below their nests.

By now, I have eased into a comfortable, rhythmic stride, stroking rapidly up the Sheepscot's middle ground. The river broadens here. Wooded coves appear well to the east, and occasional pastures are in hay on raised, tree-screened hillsides. Lehman and Woodbridge islands float to the east. A bit of the river breaks off here and arches south and then east toward Sherman Lake and Deer Meadow Brook, the narrow waterway's departure hidden by the two islands.

Both on these rivers and on the lakes and ponds that feed them are common loons. A threatened species, they are making a small comeback on Maine and New Hampshire waters. These large birds are quite social if approached quietly. I have gotten within a paddle's length of many of them and have followed along as if a member of their group once they got used to my presence. They are charming company. I am thrilled by their brilliant red eyes. In their powerful, iridescent black and white and transitional primaries, they are beautiful beyond description. After ice-out, they come off the salt water and nest alongside inland ponds, where they spend the summer trying to raise their young despite the nest damage that results from the wakes of powerboats.

Ruth Holmes Whitehead has retold the legend of Kwimu, who came from the spirit of the loon and lived among the loons. It goes something like this:

After coming ashore and taking the form of a man, Kwimu marries an Indian woman. He attempts to protect his wife and her people, but both other

Indians and white men manage to kill members of the family. Kwimu is able to protect them for seven years, often helping them slip away in silence, as loons will when disturbed. But then he must return to Kwimu'k, the place of the loons underwater. He and his wife feel great sorrow at being separated.

The loon's wife, Kwimue'skw, mourns the loss of her husband as she walks by the lakeshore. The story is retold somethig like this. The woman sees a loon person coming to her underwater. The loon becomes a man as it leaps from the water. This is her husband, Kwimu, who tells her he could not bear to stay away from her. He tells her he has returned from the waters in which the loons reside to be with her again. Thus the loons continue to commune with us in these rivers and lakes, though always remaining slightly apart.

I CONTINUE TO MARVEL at the absence of watercraft of any type moving up- or downstream. There cannot be many places on the entire eastern seaboard where one can have a whole river to oneself, but here is one in Maine. This brand of serenity is getting to be a habit. A hundred and forty miles to the south is one of the nation's largest cities. A similar distance to the northwest sit two of Canada's great cities, larger still. Portland is only forty minutes away, and the highway and Wiscasset even closer, yet the air here is clear, still, free of noise, and the river's surface, except when the breeze stirs slightly, is an endless mirror, glassy and perfect as far as the eye can see.

In his 1832 *History of Ancient Sheepscot and Newcastle* the Reverend David Quimby Cushman wrote that one of the earliest difficulties settlers here encountered was the slapdash manner in which deeds and claims to land were managed. Some early arrivals purchased land directly from Indian sachems. Others carried grant letters received via proprietorships in England, while still more came from outposts farther south, holding letters that seemed to entitle them to Sheepscot land as members of those colonies. Lands purchased from local tribal figures were not necessarily seen as legitimately owned by other leaders or tribal families. Major white landholders disputed the right of other grantees to sell or transfer property, and London frequently dipped an oar in the wrangling, making matters worse. Thus, the propelling dream of being master of one's own little acreage met resistance from the beginning.

Ahead, I can see several houses well off upstream as the river narrows and pulls westward along what locals once called Crumbie's Reach. An old truck is parked at the end of a woods road, and a man and his children fish from the shore. The river teems with fish. They leap upward through the smooth surface, do summersaults in pursuit of insects, and are back in the water before one can get a clear look at them. One could almost reach out and grab them they are so close. *Merlin's* hull seems to attract loons and fish regularly. I must discuss this with him.

Ancient Sheepscot was not a spin-off of some larger colony. It had no important patrons initially, having been charged with its own self-reliance from the start. The earliest settlement, according to cleric Cushman, was built on a neck between two courses of the river "above Wiscasset Bay." The community eventually had a main street approximately a mile and a quarter long, and its inhabitants quickly fell to fishing, hunting, farming, and building. The land in this area was held to be highly fertile and suitable for tillage.

One seventeenth-century visitor said of the river, "It sweeps through many miles of country, forms almost a countless number of acres of marsh, its waters are well-stored with fish, and its banks are lined with forests, pastures, cultivated fields and other signs of civilization." Except for the addition of a few modern homes, the scene is similar today. A burial ground was created between Garrison Hill and the Falls as early as 1630. It is there still, not far above the river. A unique experience that, being long departed yet able to listen to the river in one's deepest sleep.

In his *History,* the Reverend Cushman noted especially the cooperative nature of the early Sheepscot settlement, whose members were mutually dependent in their little society and relied upon one another. "It was a community where everyone saw that it was for his own good to promote the benefit of the whole," Cushman wrote. "Their very isolation compelled them to deeds of benevolence and to acts of common mercy and charity." Even now, the place feels like a minor Yankee Eden when viewed from the river—a village where, as another seventeenth-century chronicler put it, one could live on "the spring runs of shad and alewives, an unrivalled soil, magnificent forests and mill sites. A most desirable place." Sheepscot eventually became

The Sheepscot River at Head Tide

the garden that fed fishermen operating from Monhegan and Pemaquid, and it is easy to see why.

In 1630, there were eighty-four families in the area, many with ties to the fishing settlements of Pemaquid and St. George. Those who settled here and wrested a living from this wild place, as I have previously noted, did not formally own what they tilled. While some bought land directly from Indians, there were lords in London and "pilgrims" in Massachusetts who had other ideas about who should profit from this land. The Duc D'Rochefoucault in his *Travels* suggests that actually the Dutch may have been here first. No matter. By 1630, lords and merchant adventurers in London commenced granting disputed lands that they had never seen to certain "reliables" at home and in Massachusetts.

In 1633, the Plymouth Council conveyed twelve thousand acres here to Giles Elbridge and Robert Aldsworth, of Bristol, to settle the region. The grant, not surveyed and largely the figment of someone's imagination, more closely equaled seventy-five thousand acres. Grant or no, there remained the tough local reality of making something out of nothing on the banks of this river through immensely hard work. This same issue of land, its value and ownership, would become ugly after the Revolution when men who returned to their remote farms were told by Boston proprietors they didn't own the lands they had labored so hard to make habitable. This grossly unfair situation would later spark a second, mini-revolution in the Maine backcountry.

Those who search for such things have found the remains of a smithy, including the anvil, in Sheepscot village, along with the foundations of a meetinghouse and various dwellings from this earliest period. Sawn boards, still perfectly preserved in their sawdust, were discovered buried around the old mill site. This serene community would meet its end in the mid-1670s as echoes of the outrages of King Philip's War reached the banks of the Sheepscot. Indians began to resist the expansion of the settlements in their midst, and their trust of whites diminished to nothing. Raids increased. There were deaths and captures. Sheepscot, in its distant isolation, could not be defended. The Great and General Court of Massachusetts could pontificate, but it would not send militia to protect these remote villages. One day, while most of the

Sheepscot community were in the fields, Indian raiders set fire to their homes, killed their herds, and murdered several settlers. Those remaining were lucky to get away through the tall grass and scrub, stealing away in their boats down this same river. It would be the 1730s and 1740s before serious attempts to resettle became feasible, and hostilities would continue off and on into the mid-1700s.

THE SHEEPSCOT NARROWS from both sides four miles above Wiscasset, where a high rib thrusts out from the east side and the west shore turns and forms a pool as the river bears suddenly right. Off the end of the rib lies a rough ledge, creating a reversing falls and, at low tide, a barrier to river traffic. I have a hunch there were millwheels positioned at this point long ago. My arrival has been timed about right, and the rocky seam is fully submerged. The river's surface roils and tucks as it moves over the bar, kicking up a fine bundle of waves and froth. After exploring the pool, I set up *Merlin* for a straight approach, and over the falls we ride—no bumps, no scrapes. Then we are in another broad pool where the river makes up for its journey northward again.

This is a pretty place that invites pause. The tiny village of Sheepscot has wrapped itself around this pool and the entrance to the Dyer River, which joins the Sheepscot shortly. Steeples rise above groves of hardwoods, and a band of white pines screens a mowed field from the river. The Dyer, and the little harbor it makes, are to my right after I go under the village bridge.

An old farmhouse leans upon a hill, its surrounding pasture tumbling down to the shores of the river. I beach *Merlin* and walk up through these fields. Hay is drying in the sun on south-facing slopes. From the high ground I have a fine view back toward the center of the village, which is no more than a crossroads and some appealing old houses and, of course, those steeples.

Villages were meant to be serene places, intersections in the road where people might be civil to one another, transact their business, and anchor their experience in the presence of neighbors. I think, as I walk about in new-mown hay, of Thoreau's musing on community in numerous asides. He was displeased, one conjectures, as he saw wild places first become settled, then ugly with commerce. He would have liked this prospect, though.

In a Concord entry in *Wild Fruits,* a volume he was still working on when he died, Thoreau remarked:

> *What are the natural features which make a township handsome and worth going far to dwell in? . . . I think of no natural feature which is a greater ornament and treasure to this town than the river. It is one of the things which determine whether a man will live here or in another place.*

The scene at Sheepscot speaks to me in the same way. The river, rippled with the wind in some stretches, glassy and reflective in sheltered corners, somehow ties together this little community of spires, old houses, maple-lined lanes, and fields. The village slopes to a field above the river. Now a dense green, the field seems a park, a banner of color between river and houses. South of it, beyond a copse of hardwoods, lies the cemetery, its old stones tilted at angles induced by age and errant topsoil.

> *I think that each town should have a park, or rather a primitive forest, of five hundred or a thousand acres, either in one body or several, where a stick should never be cut for fuel, nor for the navy, nor to make wagons, but stand and decay for higher uses—a common possession forever, for instruction and recreation. . . . It frequently happens that what the city prides itself on most is its park, those acres which require to be the least altered from their original condition.*

This is the Thoreau who saw his own village disappearing into a mere marketplace, too much land gobbled up and too little left to the laboratory of nature. It is also the voice of a man ever interested in what the river and the woods could teach. At such moments, as town marched toward forest and field, Thoreau reflected on how quick his fellows were to lay waste to land in the name of a thoughtless exchange:

> *Most men, it appears to me, do not care for Nature and would sell their share in all her beauty for as long as they may live for a stated and not very large sum. . . . It is for the very reason that some do not care for these things that we need to combine to protect all from the vandalism of a few.*

A hundred and forty years later, many people are thinking on Thoreau's urging.

One can muse on what the price of preserving a river, a village, a Sheepscot, Alna, or Head Tide might be. It is, at least, resistance—resistance to mowing down the landscape to sell something, anything. Resistance to cluttering a river with the vending of junk that has no merit, and limiting riverside manufacture to those activities, such as boatbuilding, which need to be here. Resistance to the use of agricultural chemicals that may leach into rivers, despoiling them, killing fish and other aquatic life. Thoreau's concept of a village and its river is hard to find in today's world, but I find it here, on this river, easily enough today. And, I believe, so would he.

Important, fast-breaking national news was made here in Sheepscot. Not long ago, National Public Radio carried a report on the deliberations of the ladies' guild of one of these churches. The association assembled in full and formal session and decided they would no longer meet. Ever. No one does this sort of good work anymore, it appears, and the few remaining members of the guild (it was only five or six or seven) concluded that meeting further as a society would be of no avail. Thus, members of a group that had been in existence for about a hundred years went their separate ways. Not that the women would no longer devote their energies to their neighbors; Maine women of a certain age are thoroughly experienced in bringing their communities up to standard and hardly know how to rest. Such energetic souls have no truck with idleness. Henceforth their work would go on singly as circumstances required, but the formal meetings and events would go dark. The ethic here has not quite gone over to video games.

I REBOARD *Merlin* and we set out upstream. As the village recedes, the river becomes considerably narrower, tidal but not so much prey to the scouring of the current. If I paddle steadily, I will have time to reach the end of the river's navigable territory and be back down to Sheepscot again before the tide leaves me stranded on the wrong side of the reversing falls. I pass the few riverbank houses and leave behind a dock with a lone skiff. Set back in the woods on a prominent hill stands an old farmhouse. Again I have a sense of having left the settled world behind. I pass a cabin isolated in a hemlock grove. Here the Sheepscot moves through a series of marshy bends. I feel the wind begin to push from the northwest, though I am relatively sheltered at the moment. It will be a breezy ride downriver later.

The west bank of the Sheepscot resides in the town of Alna now. I dig in with the paddle as *Merlin* and I make for the village at Head Tide. The river narrows further and the banks grow higher. The countryside, except for the raised marsh that borders the stream, lies in thick woods. River, tall spartina marsh, and forest surround me with seemingly infinite shades of green. The scene is reminiscent of the west of Ireland. I pass under a power line, the only sign now of human presence. Scudding clouds of brilliant white run southeastward in a deep azure sky, the strengthening wind rolling them forward.

Watching the clock, I reach a point where the river turns more westward and into a cleft between even higher banks. Trees, knocked down by yesteryear's winds and the sweep of the current, have plunged down the banks and lie at odd angles at the water's edge. Here the Sheepscot has dug a low trench for itself over millennia. The riverbanks are littered with dry-ki, tangled root systems and whatever else the river has undermined or exposed, now left bare to the light. Something looking suspiciously like a good-sized muskrat slides into the water fifty yards in front of me. A tiny wake follows and then nothing. I have the feeling of being observed.

Maine archaeologist Bruce Bourque has searched out traces of the long, long Indian presence here. Native peoples have been established in Maine for twelve thousand years, beginning with the Paleo-Indians of the late Pleistocene. The earliest aboriginal settlers probably crossed the Beringian Ice Bridge and then worked their way eastward, eventually establishing themselves in what would become Atlantic Canada and the northeastern United States. These people left evidence of their passage in many places, and Maine is no exception.

By roughly 11,000 years B.P. (before present), nearly all of Maine's glacial ice cover had receded and a watery, stream-riven coast had formed some sixty miles inland from the present-day shoreline. Archaeological sites at Munsungan

Lake, the Magalloway Valley, and the Michaud site near Lewiston show very early settlement. According to Bourque, the landscape changed around 9000 B.P., with a tundralike ecosystem giving way to deciduous vegetation. Moose, deer, and bear moved in, and the caribou population simultaneously began to diminish.

It is no exaggeration to say that early inhabitants of the great "maritime peninsula" that is New England and Atlantic Canada brought a dynamic and innovative culture. They were people hardy and inventive enough to survive in a severe and unfriendly climate, making their way by hunting, fishing, foraging, and farming. If their way of life was primitive, it was also brilliantly adaptive. Later tribal peoples were equally resourceful.

Bourque and his colleagues have found many settlement sites from the Archaic Period, roughly 10,000 to 3000 B.P., a time of community building on inland streams and waterways, and some of the oldest coastal weir-fishing camps in America. Maine peoples adopted and modified pottery and arrow-point technologies from the South and West, too. If any people can be considered the "pilgrims" of this region that I am paddling, it is these earliest migratory groups. They were here for nearly a dozen millennia before whites arrived from Europe to "discover" this territory. Those who, in some distant way, are related to these first peoples still live here on the shores of Maine's rivers.

MY THOUGHTS return to the present as the view ahead is suddenly dominated by the iron latticework of a rather old bridge. It connects Maine routes 218 and 194, and probably doesn't see even twenty cars in a day. It reminds me of the compact Victorian metalwork span I saw years ago in the aptly named little English community of Iron Bridge. Continuing under its anachronistic strand, I curve northwestward to a point where the Sheepscot loses not only its high banks but also its depth. Here is my other reason for timing this journey; not only are there the falls in Sheepscot Village to be concerned with, there is also the small matter of having enough draft to get into Head Tide village.

The Sheepscot becomes gravelly and very shallow here. When the river's output departs seaward, this stretch can become not much more than a sequence of barely connected puddles. With plenty of rain and excess runoff from upcountry passing over the spillway at Head Tide, the river may support a craft such as *Merlin* nearly into the midst of the village, though paddling the last half mile is better done in an old ABS canoe that you are willing to batter liberally. Spring runoff, on the other hand, can fill this streambed with waves of whitewater pushing downstream in a torrent. I make it around a bend past a majestic old farm on a promontory and nearly into the midst of the collection of old houses that are Head Tide, but can go no farther.

Built in the lee of a hill and wrapped about the river, Head Tide once supported colonial-era mills of various sorts, for the natural drop in riverbed elevation here made it an excellent mill site. Rural milling was a profitable enterprise in Maine's backcountry before and after the Revolution, and competition for well-situated mill sites was keen. The records of the district show how, through money lending and foreclosure, most of the mills along this section of the river came to be owned by a single family.

Head Tide was not only the location of a natural water drop; it also made a logical jumping-off point for produce, timber and livestock from small farms and woodland operations north of here to be moved downriver. The old riverside general store remains, its shelves now empty, its handsome glass storefront denuded of merchandise. It takes little imagination to guess what this vacant place once must have been like, the pot-bellied stove glowing, farm men sitting about smoking their pipes, and an occasional hand dipped in the cracker barrel on some lost Maine winter afternoon.

The major American poet Edward Arlington Robinson was born in this enclave in 1869, though he is much more associated with the nearby Kennebec River city of Gardiner, a place that lent him inspiration and where he dwelt more or less impecuniously, his family having lost its considerable wealth in the 1870s. Robinson was in his mid-fifties before he received much acclaim for his verse. He was provided a sinecure at the New York Customs House through the influence of Kermit Roosevelt and his brother Theodore, which enabled him to write in his leanest years. In recent times, a summer poetry festival has arisen amidst his traces in Gardiner.

I get out of the kayak to stretch my legs on a big gravel bar and have a look up and down the riverbed. A bit of lunch does me good. Smoke drifts from where someone is burning brush upstream, its fragrance delightful. A lone car heading invisibly south on Maine Route 218 makes the only sound beyond the sigh of the stirring wind. This is a quiet place such as I enjoy. Some ducks wade in a downstream pool. *Merlin* needs a slight tidying up, and I remove hay and river grass from his flanks. The Sheepscot, like the Damariscotta, carries a substantial burden of pickings from along its shores. I recline on the shingle for a while, enjoying the moment. Let us tear down the shopping malls, leaving only villages with a human scale such as this. After stowing my leftovers and water bottle below decks, I turn *Merlin* in the shallows and we begin our trek back down the river.

One of the most interesting overviews of the nautical legacy of the Maine shore and its rivers is Roger F. Duncan's *Coastal Maine: A Maritime History.* Drawing on a range of local historical material, both popular and academic, Duncan details how the coast and the rivers that feed it built a long history of occupation, enterprise, and cross-Atlantic commerce. This is a saga of engagement dating back to nearly the time of Columbus, and earlier still if you include Norse and possible Irish expeditions to the Maine coast, Nova Scotia, and Newfoundland. Norse settlements in what is now maritime Canada began around 1009 to 1012, and flourished in a modest way for a number of years before intra-group strife caused their abandonment. Irish forays into northern waters pre-date modern colonization, but are difficult to substantiate.

Those who would investigate this coast and its rivers came early. Duncan notes that Giovanni da Verrazano coasted along Maine's littoral in 1524. Sailing under the Spanish flag, Portuguese explorer Estevan Gomez departed for New England that same year, and by 1525 was off the mouth of the St. Lawrence. In June, he anchored in Maine's Passamaquoddy Bay and then drifted south, exploring the lower Penobscot. Not long after da Verrazano's exploration, a Frenchman, André Thevet, visited the midcoast and traded with natives in 1555. There were certainly Portuguese fishing ships off Maine and eastern Canada during the late 1400s and throughout the 1500s, as well.

David Ingram, Francis Drake, and John Hawkins sailed from England to the Caribbean via West Africa in 1567 aboard the *Minion* and the *Judith.* Bringing kidnapped Africans to sell as slaves in the West Indies, the group got into a scrape with the Spanish off the coast of Mexico. Ingram was among those captured and released by the Spanish. Various old English documents suggest that he then made an amazing journey on foot northward from Florida on Indian trails, walking up the eastern seaboard, through Maine, and on to Atlantic Canada. He is then said to have made passage on a French ship, eventually again reaching his home country, where he seems to have fashioned a living telling the tale of his long walk for money in London coffeehouses and gin palaces.

John Walker came to Camden in 1580, and Sir Humphrey Gilbert made Maine landfall in 1584 with a fleet of five ships, a journey during which he would perish on the return trip. In 1602, Bartholomew Gosnold sailed from Bristol, England, to the mouth of the Piscataqua River, which divides Maine and New Hampshire, probably anchoring at the Isles of Shoals. Merchant adventurer Martin Pring followed Gosnold in 1603 and first came to harbor at what may have been the Fox Islands (North Haven and Vinalhaven). He traveled in the *Speedwell* and the *Discoverer,* the former a ship that would later carry the Pilgrims to Plymouth, Massachusetts. In 1605, George Waymouth sailed out of Dartmouth, possibly landing on Monhegan in May of that year. Monhegan became a major fishing station as did, later, Damariscove Island. Merely the earliest of known English and European visitors to these waters, these explorers were the first of multiple waves that would come and populate the rivers I am sampling. Duncan's review of the early history of exploration and migration suggests, as do other sources, what an important role the Maine coast and its adjacent rivers played in forging the Atlantic bridge.

MY RETURN through the upper bends goes uneventfully, the water now a bit deeper with the continuing thrust of the tide. Though I have to work some against the tidal current, the wind now has gained real muscle and rolls steadily out of the northwest and west. This morning's clear, deep azure skies have

The Sheepscot at Wiscasset

admitted a bold sun that, in turn, has heated the surrounding country, hastened evaporative cooling, and now generates rapid air movement. As the prophet said, sometimes thermals can be your friend. I am glad to find the wind off my right shoulder, more tickled still that *Merlin*'s sloped deck sheds the gusts efficiently and without complaint. It is beginning to feel a bit like September.

The river widens slowly and re-enters that stretch where it twists through tall, grassy marsh, the stream rather like a green tunnel. Ahead I spot another boat, also making southward. It appears and disappears as we all push through a series of meanders. Getting closer, I see a young couple in a canoe fighting the stiff breeze as they attempt to get hastily downriver. Wind hits the canoe broadside periodically, pushing it sideways like some infernal kite. The twosome nearly capsizes at several turnings, fighting the wind for another quarter of a mile or so, and then attempt to beach their craft at river's edge, a more or less impossible task since there is very little real firmament here, just waving spartina, muskrat tracks, and mud.

The pair appear not to need assistance, and are sufficiently preoccupied that I pass them without notice as they enact their momentary drama. With the stream all to myself, I stroke my own way rapidly down to Sheepscot's bridge and pool. Along the way, I look back several times as I paddle, but see no further sign of the couple. If they've decided to wait until the wind dies down before continuing, they will have a long, damp wait.

Gusty conditions make me question my reasons for taking to the river. What is it about wild river places, I wonder, that draws me to this kind of redoubt? Why launch into such watery backcountry places merely to obtain a certain communion with the land? Water magnifies our sense of the land. Adam Nicolson, owner of the Shiant Isles off the coast of Lewis in Scotland, has argued that islands, because of their isolation and imprisonment in water, ironically, make a person feel intensely closer to the earth. Land surrounded by water is more engaging, perhaps, because there is less of it, and we are glad to see it. I have come to agree with these sentiments, and I would enlarge them to include viewing the world from rivers.

With the seat of your pants in a kayak, you are of the river and see the passing world from an unguarded angle. That angle always reveals something of the character of a place that cannot be obtained from land. There is something *surreptitious* about quietly viewing the land from the river. Today and all my river days show me the world's back yard, its habits and peculiarities. A born eccentric, I enjoy seeing the countryside from this angle as I drift with the rhythm of the paddle. I see without being necessarily connected. I may look more closely and paddle away, or grow closer still and make terms with the shore. And, in places such as this, I can turn the boat and roll outward until, running out of river, I descend to the sea. I could continue outward there, too, if the spirit moved me. The Sheepscot allows me that feeling of stealth, of seeing and valuing secluded land from a perspective that few share. And it costs nothing beyond my own comfortable labor.

As with islands, messing about on rivers inevitably encourages a gradual turn inward, a consulting with self, to measure one's own reaction to previously unseen places, to the feel of currents, waves, wind and river bottoms. You must navigate and do the right thing, of course, gathering detail even as the boat moves inexorably forward. It's like watching a film: you collect scenes, stopping mid-current for a moment when a particular line of shore forces you to linger with its especial uniqueness. Or, a bird or an animal stealthily shifts or stands stock still, as have some of the many herons I've seen, each carefully camouflaged, something you would not easily see from land. These are the same sensations one might have had moving along this river one or two hundred years ago, tackling the current in what was then uncharted territory. Left alone, nature is timeless. Now automobile transport shields us from the new in too many ways, roads and their surroundings have become the most shabbily conventional of places. There are fewer and fewer points where we can experience the earth unvarnished. We turn to high mountains, to islands, and to rivers for this connection. There are rewards beyond movement for all this.

ONCE UNDER the bridge, I reconnoiter the falls and find them quiet, the surface moving smoothly. The tide will soon quit pushing; I need not have hurried after all. Again I've been outfoxed in my calculation of the duration of tides, but I am learning. Ah yes, I am learning. I explore the mouth of the Dyer River briefly, cross the bar a second time, and set course for Wiscasset. Two lads in play boats are waiting for the falls to begin creating standing waves again. I wish them well and run south.

It may be a commonplace to say that one sees different things on the return trip, but it holds true regardless of whether one is walking, paddling, or driving. I hug the Sheepscot's west shore to get out of the stiff breeze, which has now come around to the west and southwest. Again, the river makes its way quietly close to shore, ruffled only at mid-channel by the shuffling breeze. A man wearing a battered Red Sox cap works on his boat at a mooring. Nice day for it, he offers, and I agree. These afternoons are comfortable, the sun mellow and the prospect getting definitely fall-like. I am learning to enjoy the neighborhoods of rivers, the friendliness of people, the easy camaraderie, so different from yacht club brittleness. These rivers are not places for those playing the nautical status game. They belong to those who work them—and to the occasional interloper like me, who borrows them for an afternoon, a day, a week. When you share a river with others, you are always a local.

As I steadily descend the Sheepscot, I begin to wonder how much the wind might affect my necessary passage down Wiscasset Bay. My answer arrives fairly soon. By the time I reach the narrow section of the river above the rail bridge, the water is rough, whitecaps dot the river's unprotected eastern side out to mid-channel, and the current has become a nasty, confused muddle, to put it politely. *Merlin* begins taking sizeable waves over his bow, and the crosswinds carry rolls of whipped-up foam. I seek a vein in all this, find one, and place *Merlin* in it. We ride southward to the bridge without much complaint, but the river is sloppy and getting more so.

My new friends, the ospreys, holler at my return, circle about in question, and then drop back to their nests. (Just the sort of reaction I get when I arrive for dinner elsewhere.) *Merlin* and I slip under the old black span and down the bay's western shore. For a few moments it is difficult to make any headway, with the current still circling upriver here as it rises through the narrows. I look out over the bay. The entire expanse of this broad water is kitted out in whitecaps over troubled grey-green surf. The perspective seems less than reassuring. Perhaps I should take the bus. But there is Wiscasset at the lower end of the bay, as if just a few rods away. As I commence the downwind paddle in earnest, it becomes immediately obvious that I have an interesting and demanding hour ahead of me. The wind now comes broadside out of the southwest and west, so it offers little help and a lot of nuisance value in getting home. If I allow *Merlin* to drift very far into the main channel, the wind threatens to take us to mid-bay or even farther. I have no desire to wind up on the Edgecomb side of the bay, staring into the full force of this unwelcome breeze and a long way from dinner.

Merlin and I cling to the slight protection offered by the westerly embankment. Where it lets the wind through, we are blasted; where the cover is solid, we make a laborious headway. With the tide fully in, the bay holds its depth, and the rangy ledge I had made note of earlier now shows only its hat. High on the hill to the west is Wiscasset's ancient jail, its enormous granite blocks catching the last rays of the sun. The village is slipping into shadow, its steeples turned orange by the near-horizontal light. Much of the beauty of this scene is lost on me, however, as *Merlin* takes sizable waves over his bow again, and I paddle hard for the shelter of the bay's embankments. The wind has less effect as I near the U.S. Route 1 bridge, passing the site where Wiscasset's railroad station once stood. I never go by this spot without recalling the Kosti Ruohomaa photograph that immortalized a Maine Central night train paused at the tiny depot one winter evening decades ago.

A day's work and twenty miles behind me, I thread my way through the moorings. In the shelter of the hill, the wind drops and everything is quiet. My wander upriver has taken me from scenes of the twenty-first century to those of the seventeenth century and back again. The river was pleasant, free of modern-day noise, and, in some corners, as old and wild as it might have been for its original inhabitants and for those who arrived in the first wave of European settlement. I found two villages intact and largely forgotten (one learns in journeys of this sort the preservative value of having gone unnoticed).

Moreover, I saw hardly a living soul, proving once again that Maine rivers are good hiding places.

Wiscasset's waterfront lies nearly deserted now. Two lobstermen unload their gear at the wharf and throw the remnants of the day into the back of their pickups. I clean some of the salt from *Merlin*'s decks as best I can. Splitting and stowing my paddle, I fasten *Merlin* to the car's rooftop, and we set off for home, the sun just going down.

Day Three

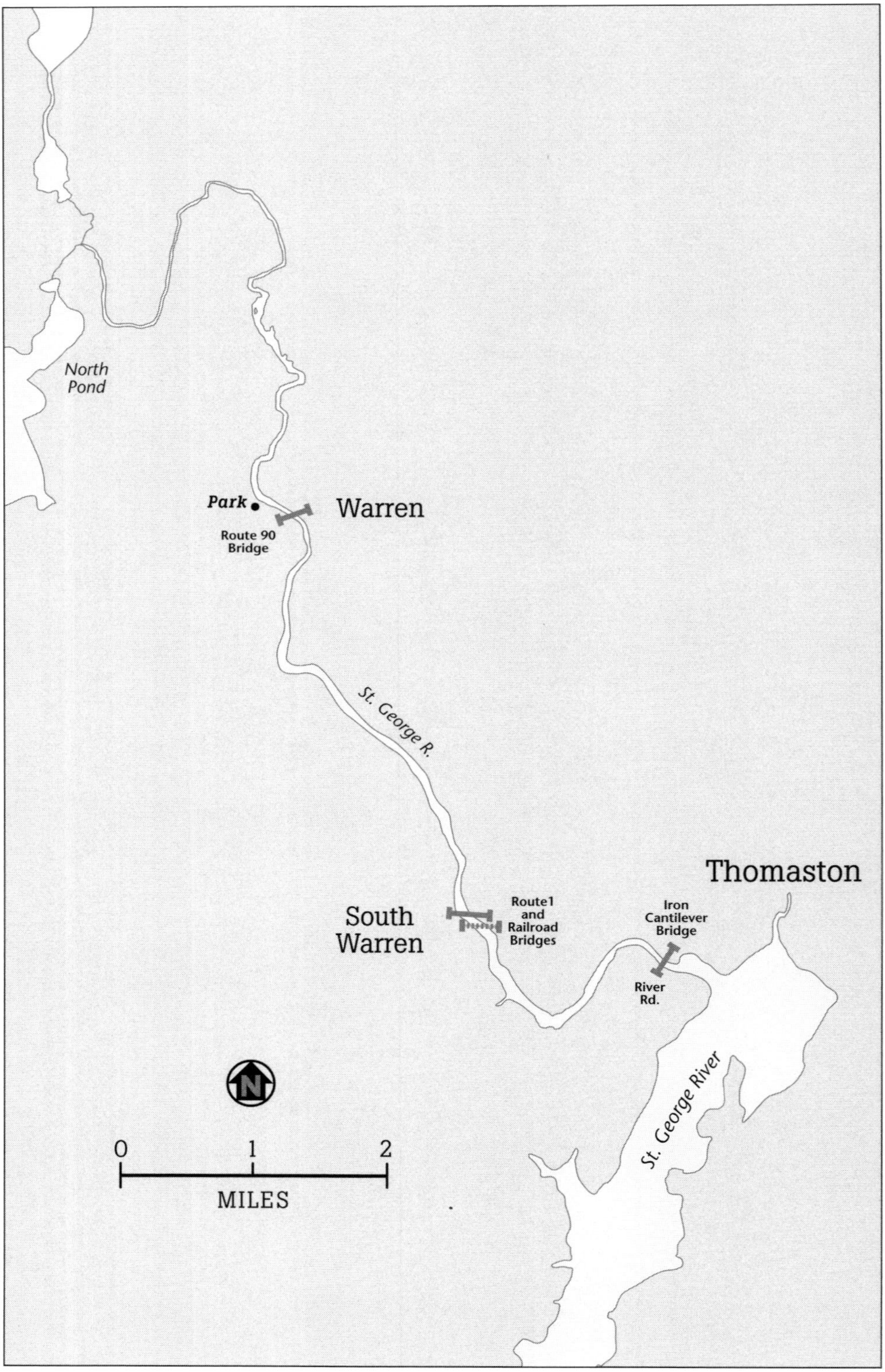
North Pond
Park
Warren
Route 90 Bridge
St. George R.
South Warren
Route 1 and Railroad Bridges
Thomaston
Iron Cantilever Bridge
River Rd.
St. George River
0
1
2
MILES

THE ST. GEORGE

To some moods, it is congenial to look over endless leagues of unbroken savagery without a hint of man.

—James Russell Lowell, *Literary Essays* (1890)

The sky looked ominously gray this morning, and it had been raining lightly. This was not good news. It appeared I would lose a day on the rivers, and I set to figuring how I would maintain my intended seven-day schedule. By late morning, however, the sky was showing patches of blue, and, by noon, the sun dutifully established itself in its usual place. Perhaps there was something to be salvaged here. Wanting to be on the water, I decided to rescue the afternoon by playing hooky and meandering up a river I had long wanted to sample: the St. George. *Merlin* was already waiting on the car, and off we rode to Thomaston.

The St. George is a sheltered, interesting river that winds seemingly forever through small towns in backcountry midway between the coast and inland cities such as Waterville and Augusta. It disappears in the midst of several lakes, only to reappear on the far shore of each, climbing northwestward. Little of this marvelous stream can be kayaked inward. There are numerous rock gardens upstream, and even covering short sections in a boat you are willing to abuse depends upon flowage levels that change often. I decide to take what I can find, and put in at Thomaston with a view to paddling the reliably navigable section, about a twelve-mile round trip up to Warren and back to this historic harbor. A pleasant way to reclaim the day and see some new water, I think.

For a warm-up, I paddle east around Thomaston Harbor, a place of both fishing boats and sport craft. Several sailboats of considerable size beat down channel toward Port Clyde and the open sea. A large marina and a restaurant are perched at the water's edge. Behind these, on a series of back streets that rise to U.S. Route 1, stand those fine Federal and Victorian homes that collectively give Thomaston the lingering look of a prosperous Maine town of one or two centuries ago. Thomaston became involved in the Revolution, its locals fighting directly with British men o' war that came up the lower St. George looking for trouble. The Thomaston militia did not disappoint them.

A heady afternoon breeze with the smell of the sea floats up the lower St. George, and everywhere on the harbor there are rolling whitecaps. The fun of looking around is compromised by the busy surf coming over *Merlin*'s deck. High time to try my luck inland. I make my way westward through the chop for the mouth of the upper St. George, which hides under an iron cantilever bridge. Hoping I will get some help from the inbound tide this afternoon, I am soon rewarded beyond my most optimistic hopes.

The current pushes upriver rapidly, and I fairly sail under the bridge and westward between the river's two high banks. This is a bit of all right. The current thrusts at about three knots, and as I paddle, I probably add another couple of knots to my speed. I enjoy the sense of speed these combined efforts produce, though there are moments when I really would prefer to go a bit slower in order to take in my surroundings. So this is how a kayak might feel if a ten-horse motor were attached. Bless you, St. George.

The river manages a sense of intimacy already; perhaps the high banks that exclude views of much of anything except brush, woods, and sky account for this. The in-sweep carries me past shelves of cordgrass, three-square, salt-marsh bulrush, and other tangled growth. Ledge shows itself as the river bends left and right gently as *Merlin* and I ride westward. Lines etched in the rock show where water has lapped high above today's levels. I wonder at the surge of tide that left marks six to eight feet higher than present high-water levels. In the years ahead, even low water levels will reach these marks as this coast becomes further submerged, the result of global warming. Twisted old trees, grey and lifeless with age and weathering, still cling to the narrow shoreline, and some grow from veins in the rock. Beyond them, the banked, dense woods are dark and quiet, birdsong the only sound. Alone in a channel where the rest of the world is away at work. A great virtue, that.

After roaming westward for a couple of miles, the river becomes expansive, and its banks to the left and ahead form a kind of high-sided bowl. The St. George widens into a broad L and turns north here. I debate whether to hug the west shore or turn more to the east side of this bay-like corner in the river's affairs. The river's surface reveals few secrets, and I gingerly make my turn, shortly finding myself spun around 180 degrees in the space of barely a second. Unwillingly, I now am heading back to where I came from.

In poking my way midstream of this bend, I've landed on the shear line of a thread of current. Bunching up on the east side of the basin and colliding with the line of tidal thrust pushing hard to the west, the conflicting currents fight for a grip on *Merlin*'s hull. The tidal force also leaches back out of the bay's west side, bouncing off the shore and kicking northward. I'm given the chance to experience what a spinning top must register. The river's movement is telling *Merlin*'s hull to proceed in three different directions, and neither of us find this particularly amusing.

I put some muscle to the paddle, moving quickly to the west side of the bend. Here the current flows more predictably and in the direction I had intended. Kayaker sentiment tends to see surfing and handling big waves as the ultimate challenge, but threading the needle in rivers where multiple currents abrade one another comes, I think, a close second. I make a mental note to plan my way through this on the downriver return. Looking northwest, I resume a more rhythmic pace, the paddle alternating steadily.

IT WILL BE clear to anyone who has traveled with me thus far that I have little affection for most things modern. I like good design, natural, undisturbed countryside, communities that are livable, and agree with the late E. F. Schumacher, who reminded us that small is beautiful. I gravitate toward the traditional, the glue of community, and freedom from the awful jim-crackery that pervades the American scene. I favor places that have evolved a sense of identity by rationally being true to themselves. It is in that spirit that I set out, and in that spirit I continue to travel, looking about on this grand little river.

Those sentiments aside, I am not a purist. One of the notions that stays

Northwest, the St. George River

with me as I paddle the quiet St. George is that, in the kind of countryside I crave, there is a place for the human imprint. Kent Ryden, who teaches at the University of Southern Maine, has argued that even the least settled corners of New England bear the stamp of human presence. In his good-to-read *Landscape with Figures,* Ryden says, "Sensing the presence of the past in nature provides a way of seeing I find rich and rewarding . . . it also feels more 'real' somehow, truer to the way that the landscape developed, more cognizant of the histories that are intrinsic to any piece of the earth's surface." The little towns, the farmsteads and old mill sites, even shrinking in ruin, are as much a part of the river scene as the forests that have grown back to hide the shape of things past.

Ryden makes a good case, I think. It is the intertwining of the human imprint with the natural world that I find continuously interesting as *Merlin* drifts from cove to cove. Ryden quotes Norman Christensen: "Even segments of a landscape that have not been directly disturbed are influenced by the human factors affecting surrounding areas." Or, put another way, the communities bordering these rivers look the way they do, even if the lands were not cut over or industrialized, precisely because humans have lived and worked hereabouts for centuries. The human imprint is discernible however modest the intrusion of small farms, boat shops, brickworks, and foundries. The shell heap I had visited on the Damariscotta was a highly visible reminder of that human presence, and the landscape was none the worse for it.

Strangely, this riverine landscape is in some ways more "natural" now than it was one or two hundred years ago. If one examines Fitzhugh Lane's nineteenth-century portrait of Camden Harbor and the Camden Hills, for example, the land is barren, unforested, and quite the opposite of what it is today. In some stretches, where human intrusion along these riverbanks was of reasonable scale and carried out with restraint, the human presence does not seem an intrusion at all, but a reasonable and appropriate fixture in the larger landscape. What Ryden describes and what I have been seeing as *Merlin* and I move along is exceptional, however, and therein lies the problem.

You can look off into the woods around here and discover the old roadbed of the long-vanished Wiscasset and Quebec Railroad. All that remains is the firmly packed soil, intermingled grass and cinders, and the brush closing in on all sides. Here and there, a tree trunk intrudes in what once was the center of the track. It seems as if the rail line vanished nearly without a trace. Its faded presence is not damaging. One can find riverside mill sites in Maine and across New England, generally, that seem merely attractive old buildings receding into the modern-day background. Many have been refurbished and are handsome architectural leaders in present-day communities. They are part of a congenial landscape.

The intrusions of yesterday were of a human scale. They made less broad an impact on the visual and physical landscape, and, with a few exceptions, have not left a ruinous blight on the land. Even the great mills of Lowell, Massachusetts, or the enormous edifice of the Amoskeag Mills at Manchester, New Hampshire, have a certain beauty. One cannot say the same of today's industries and today's merchandising. Big-box stores not only destroy the enterprises that have served a community for years, they assault the eye, epitomize ugliness, and have little continuing value to a city or town other than the ongoing vending of the stuff they sell. Big-box stores or ugly-box factories have no value as architectural features with new potential uses. We will not find their remains along rivers or in the woods one hundred years from now and remark on their continuing worth in a favorable way. The communities where these monstrosities exist will not find renewal in their wreckage. In addition, along the way, these contrary structures will have displaced existing economies and the people who relied upon them.

Today, along back roads and rivers, I find evidence that still evokes a constructive earlier America, and welcome these remnants of yesterday as a rightful presence. It is a Maine characteristic. There is something seemly *connected* about these vestiges of early New England life and commerce. Tomorrow the look back will be less pleasant, less salutary. Main Streets and the community members who staked their fortunes on doing business along those thoroughfares will be gone. I doubt we will find similar comfort again. The small craftsman industries that were once here will have disappeared. The modern manufacturing and merchandising that has replaced them will have left a much less desirable footprint. (Can you picture our descendants in 2090 rhapsodizing about the beauty of a typical 1990s roadside mall?) The truth is, it is a rare community that has saved the best of its past and let it become the engine that drives today's prosperity. It is why I would rather travel rivers than roads. As the classic architecture of Maine's traditional Main Streets has slowly evaporated, little has taken its place that is beautiful, interesting, or tied to tradition. America has torn down its bloodline. The rivers, in part self-renewing, remain.

HUGGING THE WEST SHORE, I move more northwestward past several attractive farms and outbuildings gathered above the river. Dense forest dominates the east shore, but, to my left, rolling pasture and low scrub rise near the water. It all is rather pastoral, quiet and reassuring. In another mile of easy paddling the St. George pulls leftward, first widened and then narrower, bringing me to a thoroughly rusted railroad bridge. It is a gaunt, abandoned-looking old thing, streams of flowing iron oxide imprinting its foundations. Just beyond it runs a concrete highway bridge. I follow the main channel leftward beneath it, emerging at a point where the river becomes more isolated, with few signs of human presence.

The St. George, captured by a great riverine marsh here, meanders left and right through rafts of marsh grass that divide my progress into little distances where I can see ahead only so far. The sweeping bends introduce me to a new sense of the river with every corner turned. The tide has lost much of its energy now and the surface shines like glass, its flow barely discernible. The woods come down to the stream at various points, acres of giant, old white pines slowly ceding their lives and footing to the river. The tops of several pines stand bare, their branches shedding rusty needles, their glory now reduced to skeleton-like sentry duty. Such totems are often home to the large, heavily engineered nests of ospreys and bald eagles. I paddle *Merlin* steadily northwest and, for about ten minutes, watch a pair of eagles frolicking with each other above the row of trees to my right. Their aerial maneuvers seem a combination of power, idle experiment and joyous cavorting. They slowly circle northward, staying roughly opposite my position in the winding river for a while.

I have seen no one on the river since leaving Thomaston, nor have I amidst the tall greenery of the marsh. At two or three points, at hidden bends in the river, *Merlin* and I pass an aging skiff or two, pulled up on the mud shelf and hitched to a tree. An old shack tumbles downward on a shaded knoll, probably through with occupancy forever. At one moment, New England is the scene; at another, I might be in Faulkner's Yoknapatawpha County navigating the hidden bayou south. My enjoyment increases with the miles; it is a fine thing to climb an engaging and shapely river on a late summer day. For this, I endure Maine winters.

The St. George in these latitudes is taking back the land slowly and methodically. This river plain, like those of the the Damariscotta and the Sheepscot, is broad and growing broader, the current nibbling at the higher borders of land at its edges. The pines lean into the river, their grip on drier ground undermined, their days limited. Those already fallen lay like marooned, ruined ships in the reedy shallows, their branches bleached as if ribs of aged, wooden arks gone aground. This confused detritus of limbs, broken branches, split trunks and upended roots dots the shore, especially in coves where the tide has persistently intruded. Other trunks stand like ghosts, bare, weathered and gazing out over this vast watery expanse in silence. A lone, ancient, one-room schoolhouse is barely visible in a grove of trees. Who once went to school there in so remote a place?

Nearing Warren, I pass one or two cabins lodged near the river. A large red oak has been dismasted by the wind; its upper half leans down and grazes the river by a plate of ledge. The floodplain narrows. To both sides, the riverbanks show more deciduous growth as they begin to flatten. The river surrenders the narrow groove it has made for itself in the last mile. The dense conifers yield, dark hemlock, spruce and fir giving way to pockets of brilliant hardwoods that catch the sun's light. With this alternating foliage comes a change in the very mood of the place, light and dark, young and old, simple and intricate. Limbs of hemlock occasionally extend out over the water, a blue-green fringe of delicate tracery that I can reach out and touch.

I round a bend and a row of houses appears. Beyond, some old industrial buildings are perched on the river's edge. Nothing moves. The village is quiet, the scene capable of conjuring up this place—minus autos and pickup trucks—one hundred years ago with little difficulty. I wend my way through the rock garden that lies above the mill buildings and under two bridges. It is touch and go, even with the tide flooding this hollow. A small park graces the river's west bank, and I aim *Merlin* for the shore. It is as if my arrival had been prepared for. I have this spot to myself while I relax and drain a water bottle. Occasionally, cars whoosh by on nearby Route 90.

Were it not for the boulder-strewn river course and unpredictable depths, one might continue for miles north of here on the St. George. The river moves through a host of communities—as well as Seven Tree, Round, Sennebec and Little ponds—to Lake St. George, its point of birth. At its highest point, the St. George is only a few miles from Sheepscot Pond, the head of the Sheepscot River, where I tarried yesterday. As they say, everything is connected.

I will have to bend to the paddle a little heading south, but linger long enough in Warren Village to let the current peak so I can ride down on the slack. The afternoon has cleared nicely and the day has become warm except for a tiny, cool hint of a breeze from the west. A sublime laziness threatens to overtake me. Lying on the grass and staring skyward, I could quite happily embrace indolence as a permanent thing. Waiting for the tide to ease its thrust, I take a pleasant nap with no feelings of guilt whatsoever. Most of the haste in our lives is the creation of artificial, manmade hysterias, and the stupendous illusion that the world, the entire solar system, awaits our arrival. Rivers break that habit; human schedules are of little matter where tides, wind, sun, darkness, and light reign.

It is soon four o'clock, and guilt gradually overcomes somnolence. Boarding *Merlin* again, I pick my way back through the rocks to Warren's little basin. The old mill buildings, if that's what they were, glow orange-white in the late afternoon sun. The one essential merchant in every rural Maine community vends videos out of an old storefront. I see no one about.

I retrace my path southward on the St. George now, getting a different look at things from this south-facing perspective. Soon I am back in the bends

The St. George River above Thomaston

in the marshes, but something has changed. The river is now past flood, and many of the twists and turns amidst tall marsh weed that I navigated earlier are now partially submerged. In some places, I am tempted to cut across the greenery waving just beneath the surface. Occasionally I cut a corner, avoiding a lengthy sideways excursion. The feeling of paddling in a tunnel is gone, perception of distances altered, the light changed utterly, and my experience of the journey changed, too.

HENRY DAVID THOREAU made river journeys in Maine on several occasions, tired of what he saw as increased crowding and tomfoolery in his native Concord. Thoreau found little sophistication amongst his fellow Boston and Concord citizens, and his Maine visits in 1838, 1846, 1853, and 1857 confirmed that prejudice. "The deeper you penetrate into the woods," wrote Thoreau in his Maine journals, "the more intelligent, and, in one sense, less countrified do you find the inhabitants; for always the pioneer has been a traveler, and, to some extent, a man of the world."

Thoreau could not resist comparing his Concord neighbors to the interesting people he met along Maine rivers. "If I were to look for a narrow, uninformed and countrified mind as opposed to the intelligence and refinement which are thought to emanate from cities, it would be among the rusty inhabitants of an old settled country, on farms all run out and gone to seed with life everlasting in the towns about Boston, even on the high-road in Concord, and not in the backwoods of Maine."

Upriver Maine, in the era of Thoreau's four trips to the state, was as wild a place as existed in eastern America. Outside of Portland and Bangor, it was a region of remote settlements dedicated to pulling down timber and communicating with the greater world via river steamers. A region also of moose, deer, fox, wolves, lynx, marten, weasel, and muskrat. There may have been a small remnant population of puma and caribou, as well. Some of the raw, isolated settlements that served loggers then still dot the big woods, little islands of comfort in remote corners. Log drives from these camps ended on the Penobscot and Kennebec many years ago, yielding to modern, high intensity, motorized logging of the rip, pull, and run variety. Much has *not* changed, however, for, despite heavy cutting, the land north of Bangor, if you can ignore more than thirty thousand miles of logging roads, is still in many ways like Thoreau experienced it, and the rivers are still robust.

Coming to Bangor on the lower Penobscot via steamer from Boston, Thoreau moved upstream and into the backcountry with Indian guides. He made his way into the Allagash where rivers and lakes are often one. "[W]e could not but confess the importance of a pilot in these waters," he noted. "While it is river, you will not easily forget which way is upstream; but when you enter a lake, the river is completely lost, and you scan the distance in vain to find where it comes in."

In 1846, farther upstream as he portaged his way along the Penobscot's west branch, Thoreau observed, "The evergreen woods had a decidedly sweet and bracing fragrance, the air was a sort of diet drink, and we walked on buoyantly in Indian file, stretching our legs. Occasionally there was a small opening in the bank, made for logrolling, where we got a sight of the river, always a rocky and rippling stream. The roar of the rapids, the note of a whistler-duck on the river, of the jay and chickadee around us, and the pigeon-woodpecker in the openings were the sounds we heard." He was appreciative, even amazed at the remoteness, and added, "This was what you might call a bran-new [*sic*] country." Thoreau made his first, memorable ascent of Katahdin during that year.

Maine's mystery river, its hidden waterway of the great North, is the Allagash. It is changing, of course, and logging comes very close to its wooded shores. So close that you can sometimes hear the whirr and whine of a feller-buncher as you cruise its waters. The Allagash or the St. John are about as remote as you can go without drifting into Canada. Henry appreciated the fellowship of that unusual society of people he met in the distant Maine backcountry.

In early logging days, the Allagash region was the land of horseboats, Jim Fleury, and Big Ma Tukey. Holeb Coffin brought the notion of oversized, flat-bottomed scows to the rivers of the Allagash region, not so different from similar boats used for commerce on the Susquehanna, Ohio, Potomac, and other eastern rivers. (Of course, the terrain in Maine was about as different as it could get.) More than thirty-five feet in length and nearly fifteen feet wide, the boats were pulled by a team of horses that walked up the river bottoms in water shallow enough to allow footing but deep enough to float the scows above the rocks and ledges.

A network of these scows was employed. Wagons were stationed at points where portaging was necessary, and cargo was transferred overland until it could be loaded onto the next scow at the water's edge. When an intervening lake was reached, the horses were put aboard the scow and all sailed to the next shore. Typically, men stood on the corners of the raft to guide it. One fellow either rode a tongue or sat horseback, plotting a course up the rocky streambeds. It must have been a tricky business, but was the only way to get big loads of provisions into the roadless wilderness.

William Fowler described a cadre of roustabouts that did this sort of labor, the most famous of whom was Jim Fleury, known for his muscular approach to labor-management relations. He employed a cook and general dogsbody, Big Ma Tukey. The Maine backcountry has always been a place of refuge for unconventional types who had no truck with city styles or manners. Work hard, mind your own business, and others will mind theirs. Ma Tukey was one of these characters-in-residence. She is remembered as huge, tough, and always dressed in men's clothing. Her reputation for taking no sass from anyone lingers, though there are also stories of her kindness toward those she liked. This giantess was usually seen strutting about barefoot and in a straw hat, and, according to Fowler, was described by at least one witness as having a "hell of a red nose that matched her red face." Such was the sociology of the northern rivers.

WORKING MY way southward with a leisurely stroke, I decide to take the big turn and conflicting currents on the inside. Passing the pasturelands I saw earlier, I make for the east side of the river and hug that shore as I lean *Merlin* into the turn. The river I ascended with the tide feels different now. The turn goes smoothly, the current unruffled and cooperative. The sun at my back, I cruise down the right shore as if in an aviary.

I have been continually impressed with the bird life on this stream, and I get an eyeful on my return trip. Besides the eagles spotted earlier, I have counted more great blue herons along this river than I have seen all summer elsewhere. In most of the small inlets and coves I pass, a great blue has staked out territory. I've watched them flying up and down the river edge, and now there are several perched on the branches of denuded pines, occasionally deserting their perches to swoop low over the river. Several belted kingfishers scold me, staying on a branch until I paddle closer, and then hurtling farther downstream to scold some more until I arrive there. This little game of tag goes on with one bird for ten or fifteen minutes.

Late afternoon leans toward evening. The trees behind me upstream block the light, and in the shade the air grows cooler. On the cusp of September, summer is no longer what it was. Its warmth is now merely a daytime thing. The banks on both sides of the St. George grow higher, and I urge *Merlin* on toward the girder bridge that frames the western edge of Thomaston Harbor. It has been the best kind of afternoon on a new river, and I have formed a love-at-first-sight affair with the St. George. Pleased at having rescued the day so well, I come ashore.

Day Four

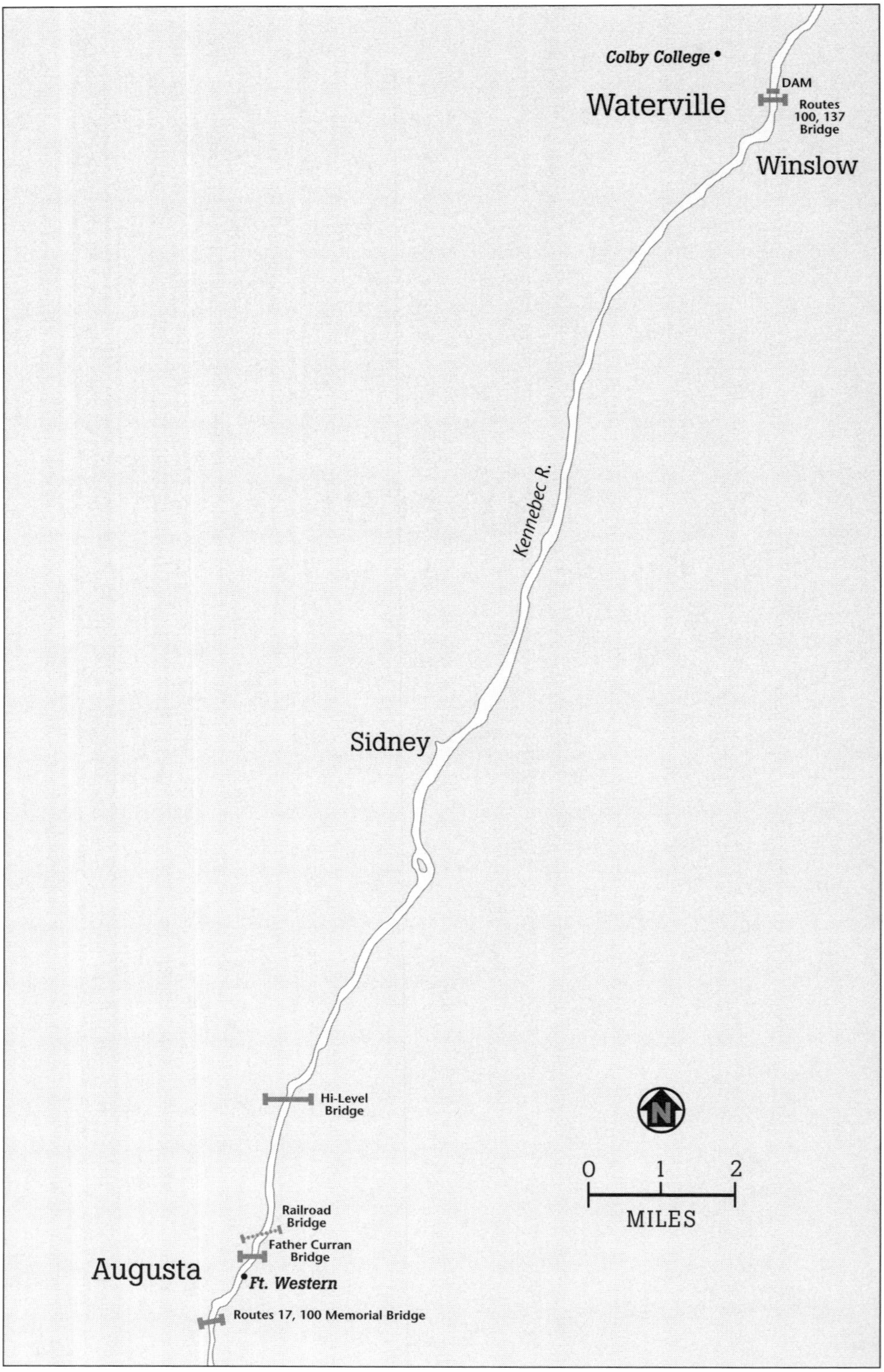
Colby College
DAM
Waterville
Routes 100, 137 Bridge
Winslow
Kennebec R.
Sidney
Hi-Level Bridge
0 1 2
MILES
Railroad Bridge
Father Curran Bridge
Augusta
Ft. Western
Routes 17, 100 Memorial Bridge

The Kennebec

Waterville to Hallowell

No employment that I am aware of threatens the life and health more than river-driving. Many a poor fellow finds his last resting place on the bank of some wild stream, in whose stifling depths his last struggle for life was spent, where the wild wood skirts its margin—where, too, the lonely owl hoots his midnight requiem.

—John S. Springer

"The River Drive," Forest Life and Forest Trees (1851)

The feisty Kennebec links Maine's great, remote timber country with the Atlantic. It drains what were the most isolated reaches of native and white settlement near the Canadian border and carries its contents to the site of America's first overwintering community on the Atlantic. Charged with the outflow of the largest inland lake on the eastern seaboard, the Kennebec finds its ageless way through miles and miles of Maine countryside, absorbing the discharge of dozens of other major rivers and streams as it roams, finally descending to the sea at Phippsburg and Popham. It is a river of contrary temperaments, at times shallow and in need of replenishment, at other moments wild and unaccommodating, overflowing its banks in the very middle of a dozen villages. I can walk down to the end of my street, reach well over my head, and show you the high-water mark on the side of a building where not-so-distant floods have left their escutcheon. With its sisters Penobscot and Androscoggin, the Kennebec empties the combined runoff of millions of acres of high northeast terrain, depositing it at the edges of the North Atlantic drift for transporting in the direction of Britain and Scandinavia.

I determine to spend three or four days on the Kennebec, working my way southward along its navigable length from Waterville down to the sea. The river is roughly 160 miles long, but heavily dammed above. I would, instead, direct *Merlin* seaward through communities of early settlement to Augusta, Gardiner, Richmond, and Bath, and then via a stretch of the hidden Back River to the lower Kennebec and the Atlantic. These were the river towns established by early British exploration, the focus of the expansion efforts of the Great Proprietors, and, later, the world's supply point for what came to be known as "frozen gold."

I launch *Merlin* in Waterville, a town of contrasts in the shadow of what Dickens might have labeled "dark, satanic mills." Waterville once boasted a range of traditional manufactures on the banks of the Kennebec, all driven directly or indirectly by river power. Like a number of other Maine communities, the town owed its birthright to the presence of a robust current and grew accordingly. Hathaway shirts lived and died here (the Hathaway label, when used at all these days, appears on items made in southeast Asia). Waterville provided inspiration for author Richard Russo's Pulitzer-prize–winning *Empire Falls.* Waterville hammed it up on its own behalf when a film production unit arrived in town to transform the novel into a motion picture not long back.

A town-and-gown place, Waterville also is home to Colby College, a distinguished small school, one of the "little Ivies." Founded as the Maine Literary and Theological Institution, Colby had its beginnings in 1818 when Jeremiah Chaplin, his wife, and seven enthused students of theology came upriver via longboat from Augusta and founded his academy near the riverside. Colby's distinctive library tower can be seen on Mayflower Hill, site of the present-day campus.

Waterville marks the limit of straightforward navigation on the Kennebec. There is plenty of water all the way north to the river's beginnings at two outlets of giant Moosehead Lake. However, the upper river is laced with dams, two of them local, some of which generate electricity. Above, there are impassable falls that require portaging, and numerous stretches where whitewater makes the rules. A burgeoning whitewater recreation industry has sprung up in the neighborhood of the Forks. You can, for a fee, rocket through the tumultuous Kennebec Gorge with others so disposed in great rubber rafts of the type often associated with the Colorado River. *Merlin* and I had modest ambitions, keeping us busy for several days of quieter paddling free from cold-water suits and capsize helmets.

TODAY, my first on the Kennebec, I will run down to Hallowell over a stretch of the river newly opened, in part, to admitting water from the river's lower reaches. Theoretically, fish are now free to swim from Atlantic Ocean habitat all the way to Waterville, where the dammed section of the river commences. Taking a last look at my surroundings, I direct *Merlin* south. From Waterville, the Kennebec drops quickly into wooded country, flows under several bridges, and rolls on toward Sidney. The ride, once I am underway, is comfortable, my effort to push *Merlin* ahead relaxed and rhythmic.

The river is wide at this point, though I am upstream sufficiently far not to feel the current that subsides just above Augusta. In spring, the river sometimes floods below here, and drifting ice dams also complicate the picture. Occasionally, unseasonable winter thaws break up the ice and cause midwinter flooding as great blocks of ice jam together at bends and bridges, each trapping a head of water. Today the weather is cooperating nicely, the late summer air sweet and inviting, the breeze from behind me.

Kennebec appears to be an old Abenaki name, transmitted phonetically as *kinbec* or *kinbequi*, among other variations. Maine tribes were offshoots of the Algonquin nation. They lived in settlements of modest size and were, except for seasonal migration, settled and tied to specific regions. The Kennebec, like the Damariscotta and Sheepscot, was a main artery of travel for tribes who lived in this region, especially the Abenaki (or Abnaki). The Kennebec was perhaps the most utilized for travel between Maine and eastern Canada as it connected with the Riviere Chaudiere via the Dead River and then to the St. Lawrence and French Quebec. Parts of the Dead and Chaudiere were impassable, so rocky were they, and a parallel route of footpaths evolved alongside their rushing waters. Canoes were pulled out and carried through the dense surrounding forest until they could be launched again with safety.

The Kennebec may have seemed more remote than its sister rivers. It did not show quite as rapid development as did its neighbors, and an Indian

Abandoned railroad bridge across the Kennebec near Augusta

presence continued even along its lower length. As part of a rough and obscure route to Canada from Boston, the Kennebec would shortly become a river that Benedict Arnold would travel. It did not early possess the burgeoning shipyards and mills that the Sheepscot and Damariscotta would enjoy. In the mid-1700s its great heyday of shipbuilding lay decades ahead as the continual series of regional wars involving the French, British, and the various tribes who joined them in hostilities waxed and waned.

As settlements such as Hallowell grew, the Indian culture was slowly elbowed into the backcountry nearby. With these changes came anger. The murder of an Indian near Wiscasset in the winter of 1749 inflamed hostilities once again. Saccary Harry, a Wawenock chief, was killed and others wounded as British seamen fired on their camp for amusement. The seamen then pushed the sachem's body under the river ice to avoid detection. The leader of the British gang was tried but acquitted in 1750. Gifts were provided to the Abenakis as a gesture of goodwill by the governor of Massachusetts. Still, many Indians remained outraged at the aggression of the whites.

In September 1755, a retaliatory Indian raid descended on Swans Island in the Kennebec. Thirteen members of the Whidden and Noble families and their hired hands were taken; Captain Whidden and his wife escaped. The captives were taken to Canada and separated. Sold to French or Indian families, some were eventually ransomed. Among these was little Fanny Noble, who survived the arduous march to Quebec and was adopted by a Montreal family to whom she grew greatly attached. She was eventually taken from a French convent school in Quebec by British soldiers, but was extremely resistant to being repatriated. (Her mother, brother, and father had visited her in Montreal, but she had recognized none of them and fled from them in terror.) Nearly fourteen, she was returned to Boston in July 1761. After a period of re-Anglicization, the returned captive married and had a successful life as a school teacher in Hampton, New Hampshire. Her story was typical of those who lived in remote river communities that experienced great risk in the years from 1675 to 1760. Many who were taken captive came to identify with their captors and later refused repatriation, preferring the life they had found with the Indians or French.

The run down to Hallowell makes its way through quiet woods and the remnants of farms and past occasional signs of enterprise. The transitions from city and town to country occur rapidly in Maine. Though the southern tier of the state is working overtime to create the same ignominious urban-to-suburban sprawl that has buried the rest of the eastern seaboard, up here there is still open country behind the malls. As I paddle, I see an osprey working the river ahead, looking for lunch. Their nests—in tall, often dead, trees back from the waters they fish—are quite impressive feats of engineering. They inhabit—and keep adding to—the same tangled platforms of twigs, leaves, and grass year after year.

IRRESPECTIVE OF THE VIEW from the river today, the Kennebec often has been a route into history. In August 1775, General George Washington held council in a large house off Brattle Street in Cambridge, Massachusetts. With him was Major Benedict Arnold of Connecticut, a rising young star in the Revolutionary firmament. Washington chose to send Arnold north, along the Kennebec to the Forks, where Arnold's contingent would take to the Dead River via the Chain of Ponds, and then the Chaudiere. Arnold's final destination was the fortified city of Quebec, held by the British then. Washington hoped Arnold could wound the English enough in Quebec so that they might yield elsewhere, shortening a stalemated Revolution.

In an unforgiving storm, Arnold sailed a small, ragtag fleet out of Newburyport, Massachusetts, to the mouth of the Kennebec, accompanied by eleven hundred men. In the rough-and-tumble of the Kennebec River mouth, Arnold's fleet contended with formidable currents, fog, stragglers, and a ship soon lost in a side channel. They pushed on upriver and arrived at Pittston, in a neighborhood I will soon be passing. There Arnold transferred his force into more than two hundred pine-on-oak bateaux built on short notice by Major Reuben Colburn at Agry's Point. The boatyard had no time to turn out the craft properly. The bateaux were built of unseasoned wood and were not riverworthy, adding greatly to the men's miseries.

Arnold's bateaux leaked so badly that more than half of the expedition's flour had spoiled by the time they reached the falls at Skowhegan. When Arnold got past the Chain of Ponds to make a leftward detour to the Chaudiere via the Dead River, he found that the latter's name failed to capture its true nature. The Dead proved to be quite alive and thoroughly disagreeable. The heavy bateaux had to be portaged repeatedly and became more of a burden than a means of conveyance. Arnold's second-in-command mutinied, stole most of the remaining provisions, and led his men to the rear. Flood waters obliterated the riverbanks near what is now Flagstaff Lake, and the Chaudiere was a half-frozen madhouse of tumultuous water and ice. Most of the remaining boats disintegrated on the Dead or the Chaudiere, and by mid-October, early snows and freezing nights attacked Arnold's remaining ragged, barefoot men. Many of them died, disappeared, or dropped from hunger before they reached Quebec, where Arnold managed to regroup the survivors and attack the fortified city, only to be repulsed.

The Arnold Expedition is still written about today, and an association exists to commemorate what was one of the bravest and most difficult military assaults in Revolutionary War history. A group called the Arnold Expedition Society is restoring Major Colburn's house on the river. Arnold, though his planned assault failed in its original intent, managed to harass the British on the upper St. Lawrence and then retreated to Lake Champlain, where he assembled a small navy to control those waters. His nagging presence there may have discouraged the British from sending an expeditionary force toward New York City via the Hudson—an accidental victory for Arnold, perhaps, but a sort of victory nonetheless.

IN THE LATE 1960s or thereabouts, Richard Saltonstall Jr. and Clinton Townsend came along a stretch of this river well above here. They put in somewhere above Anson in search of woodcock, trout, and the river itself. Their trip came on the heels of the last days of the great seasonal log drives, which were productive of both colorful legends and great damage to the river and to its wildlife. Saltonstall was writing a book about Maine, and Townsend, who at the time served as chairman of the Natural Resources Council of Maine, was trying to sell a rational plan for protection of the river's shoreline. Their journey was a kind of stocktaking, a reconnaissance, at a time when industrial abusers of this and other Maine rivers were singing their swan song even as evidence of their depredations lingered. Maine people were just awakening to the recreational and environmental promise of the state's long-abused rivers, and these waterways would be reborn with the passage of the Water Pollution Control Act of of 1972 and the Clean Water Act of 1977.

In *Maine Pilgrimage* Saltonstall described this quiet section of the Kennebec in that moment of transition. The two men saw Indian paintings on river ledges, pictures that illustrated the life of the hunter. (Other rock paintings had been lost when the timber outfits dynamited ledge to more efficiently send pulp downstream.) The Kennebec as Saltonstall and Townsend experienced it was sometimes a place of undeveloped islands, of white birch trees so big you couldn't put your arms fully around them, of black ducks and browsing deer. Of beaver lodges, and wild grapes growing in the sun. Saltonstall, who earlier had come down the East Branch of the Penobscot, found the Kennebec a more sunny, more open river, and Townsend noted that farmers still pastured cows on islands where the hay grew well.

Saltonstall and Townsend also witnessed plenty of signs of damage as they fished and paddled. The river's bed was sometimes choked with waterlogged pulpwood, the riverbanks were eroded at log dumps, slash and destruction of small growth were everywhere, and the Kennebec ran tea-colored, its waters saturated with tannin. The two men found whole islands stripped of vegetation after being run over and scoured by earlier log drives at flood. The Kennebec was not the people's river as far as the paper companies were concerned; it was *their* river—a free ride, a cheap way to debark logs, a fast way to get product to mill, where the effluent of papermaking would be discharged back into the river. Such was the ethic, such was the value system from which these rivers would have to be rescued in the years after passage of the Clean Water Act.

There were other sources of pollution, too. Manufacturing routinely dumped its wastes into the Kennebec and other Maine waters. And then there

Waterfront landing, Hallowell

were the communities, themselves. As the two paddlers were stringing up their fly rods in search of trout, they drifted past a town dump, its commingled refuse spilling down the riverbank and into the current. It was as if Mainers had so given up on their waterways that they were willing to see them as fitting places to make the junk of everyday life disappear.

New opportunity waited in the wings as Saltonstall and Townsend steered their canoe to shore above the point where the Carabassett enters the Kennebec. It was a unique time, looked at now from a distance. The river was about to regain its long-misplaced soul.

NEAR AUGUSTA, a new high-level bridge spans the river. Two giant piers climb from the current to support a graceful span. It is a long way up there, and the kayak feels quite small down below on the river's moving surface. The current pushes against the west side of the river now, and gravel bars rise opposite. *Merlin* sails merrily along with little effort behind the paddle as we encounter a wide bend and then a few industrial buildings on the hill rising from the Kennebec's east side, remnants of paper mills that have sunk into obscurity. In a state whose first livelihood has long been pulp and lumber products, the mills, large and small, are closing or reducing size. Some are periodically resurrected and falter on for a time, but the outlook isn't good. Small mills that manufactured wood products from Maine's timber have capitulated to southeast Asian competition. The capital region replaced these with computer-related manufacturing, but now those industries, too, face a precarious future. It's tough being at the end of the national pipeline.

In *Rivers of Fortune*, former Maine newspaperman and author Bill Caldwell told the story of the tremendous ice pileup that choked this section of the Kennebec in March 1896. It trapped large log booms, which cut loose when the ice finally let go, and the entire mess roared southward all at once. The breakup, which was followed by several days of driving snow and gale force winds, pushed ice and logs up into the streets of Augusta, Hallowell, and Gardiner. Water levels reached second-story windows in some streets.

The run down from Waterville is a straightforward eighteen miles, and it isn't long before I see the Augusta skyline ahead. The state capital is a city on two hills embracing the river. *Merlin* and I reach the spot where, until a few years ago, the Edwards Dam stood. The southernmost of the river's many impoundments, the Edwards trapped the Kennebec for over a century. Before damming shaped its aquatic ecology, the Kennebec supported an outstanding fishery; one can still get a sense of its lure in the stories of fabled Maine guide Dud Dean, a charming collection of Kennebec fishing tales set in another era and told by cleric Arthur Macdougall.

Rivers, however, are defenseless. With many manufacturing localities upstream and down taking power from the river and dumping heavy-duty pollutants back, the Kennebec for decades became a killing field for freshwater fish species. Not surprisingly, the Edwards Dam and others like it also affected fish spawning in the river above, despite fish ladders and other remedies. The river reached its nadir as a fishery even as factories closed, effluent began to diminish and federal water standards took hold. At last, on a sunny summer day in 1999, with then Governor King, state and national media, and some very satisfied fishermen present, a great power shovel cut away the earthen dam and the Kennebec ran free here once again. In the years since, fish stocks and spawning have improved nicely, confirming that nature will try to heal itself if we will only stop clobbering it. One would hardly know that the dam had spanned this river bend for so long; other than a small gravel shoulder on the west shore, no sign of its presence remains. A park is being constructed where the old mill buildings once stood. Dud Dean would be proud.

Augusta presents an interesting backyard to the river, its store-fronted main street showing its rear doors to the Kennebec. The Water Street stores are built high, but their cellars often flood. Merchants have learned to keep stored merchandise high and dry. The brick sides of the buildings they occupy sometimes sport old painted legends for products or services of a bygone era. A trolley line once connected the quiet state capital with outlying neighborhoods. It was often said that you could get on a trolley in Boston and, by changing from system to system, ride regional trolley lines all the way to Aroostook County.

I slide under the old railroad bridge that formerly carried grand express

Fort Western, Augusta

trains such as the Gull north from Boston and Portland to New Brunswick and Newfoundland. Its abandoned rail enveloped by brush, it is a wizened structure. Competing currents pull at *Merlin*'s hull. Concrete pylons show wear on their north sides from collisions with the tons of block ice that gather here as the river breaks up in the spring. The Father Curran Bridge is just below, on the site of Augusta's earliest ferry crossing and bridge. The first Kennebec bridge was built here in 1797. There are sturgeon in the river above these bridges. Just beyond it is the restored Fort Western, the largest place of defense and trading for British holdings on the Kennebec in the mid-eighteenth century. The fort is visible as I steady *Merlin* in the stiff current

WHEN SETTLEMENT began in Maine, the British moved up rivers such as the Kennebec and then had the chore of holding onto whatever commerce they afforded while the French pushed southward, making cause with Indians. The Kennebec brought these Englishmen particular worry because it formed part of the route to Quebec and was, thus, a potential invasion highway. This stockaded trading post forged the links of community, and by the time Arnold sailed up the Kennebec and bivouacked here in the fall of 1775, Augusta was a settled place. Fort Western celebrated its 250th anniversary in 2004, looking backward as is desirable at such moments.

I steer *Merlin* to the east bank, bvelow the fort, and clamber uphill to that flat plain on a promontory the Indians had dubbed Cushnoc. Long, high walls of palings form the outer defenses around the fort, and blockhouses guard its corners. Coming out to meet me, Museum Director Jay Adams explains the fascinating history of this very old place as we walk along the defenses. Jay's enthusiasm and modestly encyclopedic knowledge of Kennebec Valley history carries me along as we later tour through the main house and its varied exhibits on the fort museum's major themes: military defense, storekeeping, timber, and furs.

In August 1765, William Lithgow, who lived upriver at Fort Halifax, at the junction of the Kennebec and Sebasticook rivers in what is now Winslow, journeyed down this stretch of the Kennebec in the company of four Norridgewock Indians. Jay shows me some of the contents of Lithgow's journal where he described the journey, including his coming ashore at Cushnoc, or Cusinock, "the head of tide," as the Indians named it. On a point of land in the Kennebec, Lithgow and his companions found this fortification, constructed in 1754 by the Plymouth Company and its heirs and assignees. Fort Western had been built as both an entrepreneurial and a military venture.

The river ledges just above present-day Augusta wouldn't permit entry for the large sailing ships or schooners that came upriver from the Atlantic, so Cushnoc became the staging point for holding and reshipping goods upriver to Fort Halifax. Thus, Fort Western grew as a center of trade and supply as well as a garrison, its commercial importance expanding and diversifying even after the British gave up the river. The settlement operated under the aegis of the Kennebec Proprietors and then passed into the hands of the Howard family, and, in the Victorian era, was remodeled and became immigrant housing.

Surrounded by the sporadic actions of the French and British and their Indian sympathizers, Fort Western nonetheless avoided direct participation in the rolling conflicts that beset Maine from the 1670s to 1769. The British left the garrison to its fate, and the main fortifications decayed or were torn down. The main barracks house survived, with the general store's business being kept on by James Howard, who resided in the large structure from 1781. The fort underwent a first restoration in 1922 with help from the Howard heirs, and a second restoration in 1987 replaced outbuildings, picketwork, and the parade ground. Today, Fort Western, owned by the City of Augusta, is America's oldest remaining wooden fort and was listed as a national historic landmark in 1974.

Jay tells me that, after 1769 and the fall of Quebec, the Kennebec Proprietors offered 250-acre farms to those who would settle here. Many French Protestants, fleeing the turmoil of religious friction in their native country, were represented amongst the earliest settlers. As settlement grew, however haltingly, the fort community was required, perforce, to become productive, both on its own behalf and as a means of affording imported goods from England. Timber was cut and milled hereabouts, shingles were produced, barrels were manufactured, and a retail economy based on essentials developed. The commercial side of the fort, the real interest of the proprietors, became the nexus of manufacture, trading, storage, and milling.

Massachusetts had seen the fort as a means to control or regulate river commerce and to prevent further French encroachment from the north. The Kennebec Proprietors were content to build a cadre of *arrivées* and to do business with them. As more settlers arrived, farmsteads pushed farther back from the Kennebec, and Cushnoc evolved into the largest upriver community of its day.

"There is so much here, so much that we want to share, all these symbols of what life was like in a frontier world," Jay comments. He is an avid promoter of seeing regional history firsthand. Visitors of all sorts make their way to this exceptional fortification, especially in summer, and students from schools and colleges visit during the academic year when mere history books will not do.

Jay talks about the Howard family, whose influential scion, James, became a justice of the peace in the 1760s and a major grantee by 1771, eventually owning well over twelve hundred acres locally. Howard and his heirs operated the fort store for more than fifty years after the Revolution, and conducted a shipping business to Boston. As I stroll through the old house I get a sense of the life lived by those who risked everything to wrest a life from this region two centuries and more ago.

My interlocutor is busy preparing the 250th-year celebration of the fort-as-museum when I visit, and I have more miles to paddle today, so I bid my goodbyes to Jay and head for the river, knowing I will return before long to soak up more of the flavor of this ancient riverside place.

MERLIN AND I turn south once more. Just south of the fort is Augusta's Memorial Bridge, which makes a soaring diagonal over the river. The streambed worn by the river here is very deep compared to surrounding bluffs, though actual river depths even at full tide are modest. The Kennebec has etched a trough for itself, meaning that any efficient span here must depart from a height of land, travel at an exaggerated height above the river, and then land on another high point at the other side. This has resulted in some impressive bridge design and engineering. Sliding past the massive, two-story-high concrete footings that support the girder legs of this airy structure, I paddle along the river's west shore toward Hallowell, where I will leave the river, calling it a day.

The river was the only real connector between Augusta and Hallowell in

1775 when Dr. Isaac Senter, who accompanied Benedict Arnold's expedition as a field medic, attempted to stroll overland from one settlement to the other and complained irritably of the utter absence of any walkable route between the two. If he, in a premonitory moment, knew what lay ahead upstream for himself and Arnold, he might cheerfully have settled for what he found here.

The channel stays to the right as I glide by a series of gravelly shoals opposite that become high and dry at low tide. They are the first of a series of raised shallows that follow the shape of the Kennebec's east shoreline for some distance. Even as recently as the Civil War, military types considered defense of this river section prudent, and on the east bank stand two classical granite structures built for garrisoning the shore. The buildings, which are being readied for new uses, display the reserved, timeless lines of Hellenic architecture.

We pass another gravelly bar, Britts Shoal, as we hug the brushy, banked shore opposite. A series of buoys pitched in the channel here mark the narrow, ten-foot-deep passage. The river jogs to the west and Hallowell lies ahead, draped over a hillside. Steeples escape the shade of hardwoods. The rooflines of a raft of old houses—Federals, Colonials, and the occasional Gothic edifice—greet the eye. I paddle onward to the town's little waterside park and boat ramp. People tell of good fishing in the cove just below here.

To pass the short bit of riverbank that is Farmingdale and continue on to Gardiner would be but a straightforward drift past Shepard Point and Vaughn Brook, but that can wait until tomorrow. The sky is darkening to the west, and a light, deceptive breeze arises. I expect rain and guess that it won't be long in coming. The usual day's-end chores occupy me for twenty minutes or so. Large drops of rain fleck the windshield as I drive away from the river.

Day Five

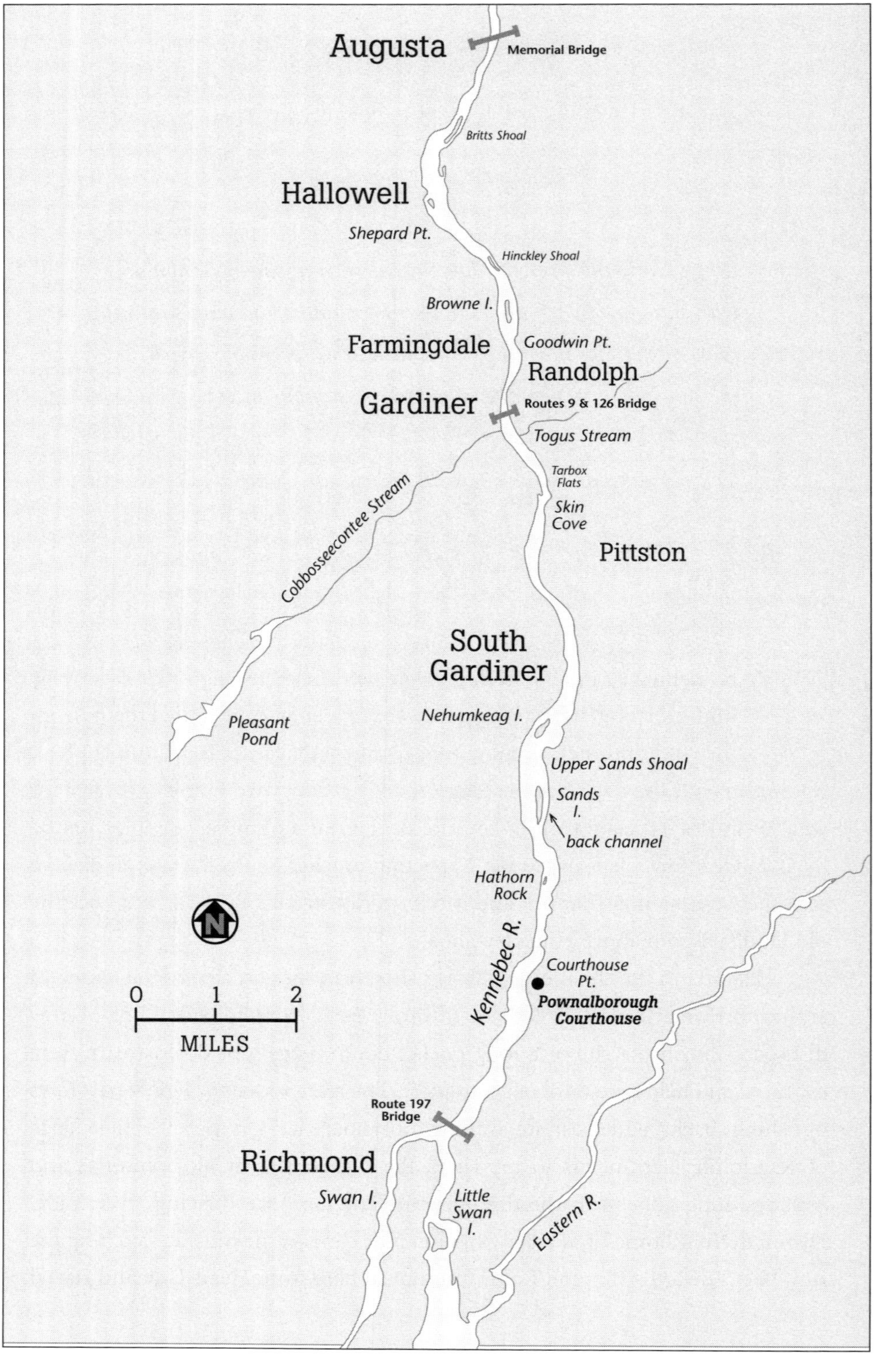

Augusta
Memorial Bridge
Britts Shoal
Hallowell
Shepard Pt.
Hinckley Shoal
Browne I.
Farmingdale
Goodwin Pt.
Randolph
Gardiner
Routes 9 & 126 Bridge
Togus Stream
Tarbox Flats
Skin Cove
Cobbosseecontee Stream
Pittston
South Gardiner
Nehumkeag I.
Pleasant Pond
Upper Sands Shoal
Sands I.
back channel
Hathorn Rock
N
0
1
2
MILES
Kennebec R.
Courthouse Pt.
Pownalborough Courthouse
Route 197 Bridge
Richmond
Swan I.
Little Swan I.
Eastern R.

The Kennebec

Hallowell to Richmond

Down along the river the doors stood open in the big icehouses, with sides lined with sawdust, that for months had been shut in silence except for the sharp, thin music of wasps. Men were clearing out old roughage and rubbing the sections of track free of rust. Machinery was being oiled. Gouges and scrapers were being looked over and assembled by the river's side.

—Robert P. T. Coffin,
Kennebec, Cradle of Americans (1937)

The Kennebec is silver today, bright with reflected light. Underway by mid-morning, I am looking forward to seeing some settled towns from the river and then slipping into territory that is more secluded. I load up *Merlin* with the day's few necessaries, taking along two bottles of water for what promises to be a warmish day. The sky is clear and merely dappled on the horizon with tiny wisps of clouds. Expecting to paddle into the sun all day, we seek the west-leaning channel, and *Merlin* glides steadily by what was once the old Dudley Boom above Hinckley Shoal.

I stay with the channel as it works shortly to the east side of the river and around Browne Island. The lee side of Browne is decorated with a line of now disused cribs on the site of a long pocket boom. Logs sent downstream were captured and held here until taken to mills. The river widens as I glide past rows of fishing shacks hauled ashore, waiting for January ice. On my left is the village of Randolph; Gardiner is to my right, the former site of old icehouses and wharves, long gone with the disappearance of the once thriving river trade. Distinctive old homes and a bevy of churches cling to the hillside, catching the sun. Poet Edward Arlington Robinson moved here from Head Tide and stayed on in the journeyman heyday of his most active writing years. In his writings, Gardiner was "Tilbury Town."

Moving under a concrete bridge, I pass Gardiner's beautiful old Maine Central Railroad station and skirt the point where Cobbosseecontee Stream empties into the Kennebec. This is the finish line area for the annual Great Kennebec Whatever Race. Nearly anything that floats is allowed to participate, meaning that bathtubs, rafts, barges, pontoon-based outhouses, and other impedimenta of the rural life are all launched and paddled in haste from Augusta to Gardiner, all in hopes of not only winning but of simply staying above the river's surface. Capsizes, partial sinkings, and even total disappearance of some craft are a regular feature of the competition.

Beyond, I navigate more southeasterly as the commercial districts of both towns begin to slip away. We pass the outlet of Togus stream and, nearby, the old roadbed of the long-abandoned Kennebec Central Railroad, a narrow-gauge line that connected the river and the Togus hospital, the first veterans' hospital established in the United States (1866). Maine once had a little railroad for almost every purpose.

Keeping toward the left bank, *Merlin* and I stay in deeper waters and pass Tarbox Flats and Skin Cove. Somewhere here, along the east shore at Agry's Point in Pittston, Major Reuben Colborn built the two-hundred-odd leaky bateaux I have mentioned and Arnold's men rode them upriver. The officer's old house still stands on a rise, and I have explored its rooms. How cold these old timbered, horsehair-plastered houses must have been; occupants needed to keep a fire going in the grate at all times except during sleep. The fires were banked at night. Arising in the mornings must have demanded a kind of Stoic courage.

THE RIVERS, bays, and harbors up and down the Maine coast have for centuries been repositories of supernatural belief. I think of that as I drift downriver. Superstition once held that if, as a sailor's journey began, the first individual he encountered was female, his luck would turn for the worse. Another widespread notion was that carrying a small stone of jasper in one's pocket would prevent drowning. Tuesday was deemed an unlucky day to weigh anchor. I've attempted to stay on the good side of these situations since the time I rolled out of bed this morning.

Horace Beck, in his *Folklore of Maine*, collected the story of a vengeful witch who frequented the waterfront. A local fisherman made the mistake of entering into argument with this woman and earned her wrath. The witch made it clear to him that he would regret his attitude.

Later, when the man went to haul his traps, he found a large coal-black hound sitting in the bow of his battered dory. This big, menacing animal foretold bad luck, which the fisherman was eager to avoid. The hound would not leave at his command, and growled fiercely. For several days the man didn't dare put to sea to haul. With no catch, he lost his meager income. When finally he could wait no longer, he got his shotgun and fired a blast of rock salt at the hound. The dog disappeared. Within the hour, the fisherman learned that the witch woman had been mysteriously injured by gunshot as she sat before the fire in her house.

And then there is the story of Judith Howard, who lived in the neighborhood of Cundy's Harbor. She may have been a witch, and at the very least possessed a powerful spirit. The old woman demanded certain burial concessions when she passed on in 1768, insisting that she not be buried near the grave of an Indian whom she disliked. Her deathbed request was ignored by her townsmen, who placed her in the earth next to the deceased red man.

Soon, the villagers paid handily for their indiscretion. A disgruntled Judith Howard would not let them rest. The animals of the village howled and fought all night, screeching and barking. Buildings creaked and groaned. Doors slammed loudly in the dark. Cows refused to give milk. It's said that the nightly din continued until the townspeople dug up the old woman and hastily transported her to burial some distance away, when at last peace descended.

The most interesting story retold by Beck is the often-repeated tale of an ancient woman who lived on Burnt Island at the coast. Anyone who fell afoul of her sooner or later regretted it. She was reputed to be so in league with Lucifer that she was unable to recite the Lord's Prayer. In Beck's version of the story, the

Bend in the river—the Kennebec at Hallowell

witch could not keep her shoes mended; they willfully fell apart once worn, so powerful was her magic. She once sat on a knife blade and shattered it.

There came a day when a seaman argued with her. The old woman warned him he'd regret the insult. When he rode past her house one day in his horse and cart, his horse suddenly reared up and would not pass. The horse's leather harness fell apart and lay on the ground, threadbare. The nautical chap was left with a wagon to push home, while the old woman stood in her doorway and hollered that this was his comeuppance.

THE RIVER straightens below the Agry's Point, warps eastward, and then begins a long arc of several miles, gradually working its way westward as it goes by South Gardiner. I see few other craft on the water here. The east shore is densely set in evergreens, mainly hemlocks, and is interrupted only by a small marina. A little-used rail line occupies the high banking to the right, its telegraph poles crumbling landward in tangles of copper wire and greenbrier. An occasional car drifts by on Maine Route 24. This section of the river has a Maine flavor: few dwellings, ledge, dark water, and horizon-to-horizon conifers. Taking the inside channel, I paddle beyond tiny Nehumkeag Island and on past Goodwin Point, which juts from the east bank.

The reassuring fact that I am making my way along one of Maine's major rivers without seeing *Merlin*'s hull coated with oil slicks, industrial effluent, floating sewage. and garbage is a modern-day privilege. This is a recent boon. Waterpower was plentiful and cheap from the time of settlement, and industries flocked to Maine's rivers, using the current to run their mills, first directly and then via power generation. They also threw their manufacturing offal out the back door, where it conveniently disappeared. It is hard to say no to pollution when a paycheck comes with it, and for decades Mainers uncomplainingly watched their streams grow filthy. One of the most well known indicators of the toxic chemical filth of these rivers was that in many communities the fumes of effluent routinely ate away the paint on riverside buildings.

The polluters were not merely the Boston- and New York-based factory owners of yesteryear. Their supporters lolled in state government, the banking business, and local politics. As recently as the 1990s, a Maine congressman—who was elected to the astonishment of his own party, to say nothing of voters—speechified on Earth Day that we didn't need environmental laws because companies had always done a commendable job of policing their own environmental matters. This was the worst kind of foolishness, of course. It was the federal Clean Water Act of 1972 that brought an end to dumping everything including the kitchen sink into Maine's rivers, not the generous spirit of absentee factory lords or their political shills.

Then there was the man who owned a septic system cleaning business near the Damariscotta River whose puzzled neighbors wondered where he was dumping all that stuff. Authorities eventually found out: The man simply waited until dark and then dumped it by the truckload into the river. Even as most of us were thinking about restoring these rivers to be something like what they were in the days of discovery, this brilliant fellow was doing his best to maintain a new standard of filthiness.

The problem of valuing rivers as something more than just a dumping place is not new, of course. More than a century ago, author Sarah Orne Jewett, a South Berwick native who grew up on the banks of the Salmon Falls River, lamented the spoliation of Maine waters that came with the spread of manufacturing. In 1881, Jewett, who penned the timeless *Country of the Pointed Firs*, assailed the creeping ruin of inland fisheries through overfishing and pollution in *The White Rose Road*. Jewett wrote of how fish had once been so thick on her local rivers that "you could walk across them below the falls." However, the times were changing, and not for the better: "[G]ood river fish are growing very scarce," wrote Jewett. They would grow scarcer still. Other individuals raised their voices, too. In *The Maine Woods*, Thoreau had already spoken of the American tendency to look elsewhere for its cues. He believed his compatriots were still looking outward to Europe and Asia for their models, unmindful of their own rivers or forests, and going "to the West Indies for their groceries."

Americans had missed the value of the rivers and forests right under their noses, Henry thought. "[O]nly a few axe men have gone upriver into the howling wilderness which feeds it," he wrote. "The bear and deer are still found within its limits, and the moose. . . . Twelve miles in the rear, twelve miles of railroad, are Orono and the Indian Island, the home of the Penobscot tribe, and then commences the bateau and the canoe, and the military road; and, sixty miles above, the country is virtually unmapped and unexplored, and there still waves the virgin forest of the New World." It is as well that Thoreau did not live to see the industrial forestry and large-scale papermaking, tanning, and other processes that took their toll on Maine rivers after his passing.

Maine people have since gone on enthusiastically to support protection of their rivers and bays. The work is far from complete at present, but good fishing has come back on some rivers, including this one, after being nearly destroyed. There remains the problem of numerous dams, most of which do not generate useful power but merely constitute obstructions to river recovery and restoration. Meanwhile, the efforts of various environmental groups, of sporting organizations like Trout Unlimited, and of local citizens have made an enormous difference. All of us who would make a journey such as mine owe those people a thank-you—and our own eternal vigilance.

JUST BELOW the small settlement of South Gardiner, *Merlin* heads west with the channel as the river makes a broad, sweeping bend around an island impoundment once used as a kind of natural pocket boom where logs could be held temporarily. Here lie Upper Sands Shoal and Sands Island. I work my way along the length of this north–south bar behind which is a channel now silted-in at its north end. Curiosity gets the best of me; a brief exploration of the back channel might be gratifying. At the south limit of this variously wooded, turnip-shaped island are the stone cribs that, linked by chain, once held the boom in the back channel until it was time to release the wood. Clusters of small hardwoods grow from the top of these rock piles, their seed carried here by wind, water, or birds. The cribs resemble nothing so much as oversized plant pots that have yielded not roses but whole trees.

Turning northeast, I paddle up the back channel, taking some time out to inspect this little hidden world. A great blue heron rises soundlessly from the water ahead of me, an avian 747 lumbering skyward on oversized wings,

Old log booms in the river—the Kennebec at Farmingdale

stroking northward. After a couple of hundred yards, depth becomes so shallow that I can't get any grab with the paddle. I negotiate a turnaround in thick marsh grass and am spared running aground. If the river, itself, was quiet, what I encounter here behind the island is absolute serenity, the only sound emanating from birds along the wild eastern shore. One could hide here indefinitely, unseen and undetected. The cove is a place of watery abandonment.

IN THIS AGE of electric conveniences, it is hard to countenance the notion that once one of Maine's largest businesses was frozen water. This is not said in jest. As I navigate down the Kennebec, I watch for any remaining evidence of this formerly dynamic industry alongshore. Even now I am making my way along a section of the river that, at one time, was densely flanked by icehouses. Maine ice, particularly Kennebec ice, went all over the world, prized for its purity and blue-white color. One might argue that while France purveyed wines and perfumes to the world, Maine settled for timber, ships, fish, and millions of tons of export ice. Therein lies some history.

The surfaces of the Kennebec, the Eastern, and other adjacent rivers predictably generate thick ice in winter. A longstanding tradition of ice fishing on the Kennebec and Eastern still lives. The lamps and little stoves in fishing shacks clustered together in favored coves give off a glow if you see them on a winter night.

Though the rivers I am traveling are occupied at their lower ends every twelve hours by salt water, there is a limit to how far the tongue of salt current reaches upriver. Since the ocean is seasonally colder and denser than the fresh waters flowing downstream, salt water is overridden by fresh, and this interface usually occurs somewhere within a few miles of the Atlantic.

The salt tongue pushes to the bottom and no farther, and, in winter, the fresh surface water freezes solid upriver from this point of contact. For each river, there is a zone where this transition occurs; on the Kennebec, it lies around Bath a couple of miles below the Chops. The when and where of the freeze varies each year. There are even years when a thick, solid surface melts in several uncommon days of warm rain and then freezes hard again for the rest of the season as more typical temperatures return. Each year freeze-over time is slightly different, but at some random moment, temperature overcomes movement, salinity, and the shelter offered by streamside vegetation, and the river surface freezes.

During the 1870s, an enterprising Boston merchant decided that Kennebec ice might be a profitable thing, bringing a sense of businesslike organization to an informal trade that had been conducted by small operators between Maine and the West Indies. By 1900, there were forty-seven ice-harvesting operations in three counties scattered along the Kennebec from Pine Grove at Bowdoinham to the Coney and White plant in Augusta. Each of these frozen-water harvesters had large storage facilities that held ice in multiple houses, each holding many thousands of tons.

Small communities actually developed at some harvesting points, like Oak Grove in Dresden, where there were large boarding houses for workers, horse stables, farms for raising produce and hay, farriers, and workshops for toolmakers, carpenters, and makers of other accoutrements. Workers who were not accommodated on site boarded with families on nearby farms. The work was seasonal, of course; the cold misery of scraping, cutting, and storage in winter, and the heavy work of loading and shipping in spring and summer provided a typical wage of seventy-five cents to a dollar a day.

Men from many surrounding farms and villages came to work here on the frozen Kennebec, first on the erection of the icehouses and then in the harvesting. The Reverend John Beedle of Dresden worked on the building of a nearby icehouse, farming and preaching in his off hours. His family gladly took in boarders and apparently was not above a little proselytizing while they were under his roof. Beedle wrote in his diary of March 20, 1870: "The turnout at our prayer meeting was very small this evening—only myself. Many are sick with the *ice fever*, I hope when the ice is out they will get better." On March 12, he had written, "The weather continues warm but still the ice is run into the buildings along the shore, they will soon get through, they work until 12 o'clock at night—the most of my boarders work until 12 midnight." And, on March 25: "Our boarders are all gone this eve helping to get in the ice. They think of running all night or until they get the house full. I hope the ice fever will abate pretty soon." Perhaps they were at pains to avoid the Reverend's preaching?

As Jennie Everson recalled in her wonderful *Tidewater Ice*, the frozen water industry required the agencies of a complex hierarchy of jobs, each essential. There were area bosses, elevator bosses, house stevedores and house bosses. Watchmen, who also tended lanterns, blacksmiths, hostlers, and carpenters looked out for animals and buildings. Then there were the common icemen who cut, dragged, and pried loose the ice in harvested grids. Since all ice was sent outward on sailing ships, men who worked the nautical world joined those who discharged ice, come shipping time. The ghosts of all these and others crowd the river.

A complex sequence of events occurred once the ice was deemed ready for capture. In the harvesting months, grids were marked and grooved on the ice after scraping, canals were cut leading to the ice elevator, and rows and blocks were cut using handsaws, busting bars, and chisels. The ice, floated down the miniature canals to the elevator, was then hoisted to a particular floor of an individual icehouse for storage.

This was not only cold work, it also could be dangerous. Beneath the frozen surface, the Kennebec kept moving. Fractured ice, often in large blocks, might move and roll under the surface ice, jamming and cracking the surface layer. Ice jams could tear away wharves and equipment. Constant vigilance was required to keep these structures clear. And, as rows and blocks were cut and moved, gaping holes over open, racing water became a hazard for men working around them, particularly at night in temperatures of twenty below zero. Watchmen marked the boundaries of open water with lanterns as a warning. To fall into a hole was to be swept quickly under an adjoining ice sheet and downstream, immune from rescue. In the icehouses, constant danger lingered where an arm or leg might be caught in a conveyer or pinned between moving blocks of ice. The income the ice industry provided made a difference on rural farmsteads, a rare moment of actual cash money, but it was a rare man who said he looked forward to a twelve-hour shift on the ice with the wind howling.

Refrigeration killed it all, of course. When the Kennebec ice industry got underway in the 1860s, most thought they had stumbled onto a never-ending source of income, a commodity free for just the taking and shipping. A golden egg, if you will. Hot places all over the world would forever hunger for shiploads of cold Maine ice, would they not? For a while, their expectations seemed justified. Then some wise soul conceived the principle of the heat pump and realized that it could be enlisted to keep food and water cool. Soon after the turn of the twentieth century, the industry began to decline, and by the 1920s, icehouses were abandoned—stripped of their timber, burned, or left to collapse. People went back to the woods or farms. The Kennebec ice era mimicked the Alaska gold rush—suddenly it was gone.

I PUSH SOUTHWARD in the main channel, keeping to the west shore. There are hardwoods now; birch, beech, and red oak climb the steep banking. The river holds its quiet. Only two powerboats have passed by all day. It is comfortable to just fall into the rhythm of the paddle stroke, moving steadily toward the horizon, *Merlin* accelerating easily along the smooth surface. Well ahead, near Hathorn Rock, I see a good-sized shape that must be a hawk or an owl in a streamside tree. It offers its large back to me in silhouette. Paddling for another five minutes, I draw near the large, perched form. It decides I cannot be allowed to get much closer and rises in flight. Immediately, a great cacophony of angry yelping comes from an unseen host of crows in a grove of trees adjacent. My new acquaintance, which I can now see well enough to recognize as a red-tailed hawk, has apparently been menacing their communal branches. The crows remained still so long as their adversary merely stared at them, but in flight he became intolerable and they mobbed him, forcing a landing a few trees away. The standoff resumes, the squawking subsides, and I pull away.

One of the standard axioms of kayaking is to dress for the water, not the air—meaning, simply, to wear clothing that will keep you adequately warm if you capsize. This is not as easy as it sounds, for the air may be warm or even hot on a summer paddle, while water in rivers proximate to the ocean can be very cold, especially on an inbound tide. Spring days, when the air temperature may be in the sixties, often see coastal water temperatures in the high thirties or low forties. If everyone were to adhere closely to the standard rule, we would always be clad in a foam wetsuit or a drysuit, both uncomfortable, the former clammy and bulky, the latter awkward and very expensive.

Today it is warm enough to paddle in short sleeves, and the water temperature this far up the river is merely cool. No need for a wetsuit, and the boat is getting uncomfortably warm beneath the spray skirt. My "flotation device" leaves me feeling rather swaddled and hot. There seems to be a version of Murphy's Law that guarantees that if you paddle rivers in the sun, below decks you get moist heat. This is less of a problem in the open ocean, of course, where sea water on the hull acts as a refrigerant. While my upper body catches a bit of breeze, beneath the skirt, the direct sun has created an undesired sauna. Pulling back the spray skirt, I let some cool air into the cockpit and allow my legs, which resemble unsuccessfully poached salmon, to dry off, a ritual I've repeated numerous times as I paddle this week.

MY DESTINATION, Richmond, is a couple of miles south yet, but I have an intermediate stop to make on the east side of the river, in Dresden. I watch the east shore for the imposing shape of the Pownalborough Courthouse. Beyond a series of shoreline outcrops, I eventually spot Courthouse Point leftward and downstream. With another quarter hour of paddling, *Merlin* and I slide toward the gravel banking behind the great, old mansion. There is no public dock here, not even a good place to land. I manage to exit *Merlin* and fasten him to some bushes without disgrace, and scramble up the steep banking.

The watery neighborhood of Courthouse Point has an interesting legal history. In 1761, the Kennebec Proprietors who had assumed royal patents to lands along the river began to exercise control over the region. Boston housewright Gershom Flagg was selected to build a courthouse here in what was then called Pownalborough, and the grand Federal structure that became court and judges' chambers, household, tavern and meetinghouse resulted. This building was originally within a stockaded fortification armed with four cannons. The Inferior Court of Common Pleas and the Court of General Sessions met here,

Pownalborough Courthouse

its justices drawn from the regional gentry, men of probity but usually without legal training.

In major cases, legal minds from Boston came here—men such as John Adams, who argued in this court occasionally in the years before his ascendancy. Adams first made the very difficult journey to this remote chamber in 1765. William Cushing, later Chief Justice of the Massachusetts Supreme Court; James Sullivan and Increase Sumner, both of whom later governed Massachusetts; and Robert Treat Paine, a signatory of the Declaration of Independence, followed Adams.

The cases tried in this building emphasized the religiosity and correct conduct of the period—a time that, on reflection, one might be glad to have missed. Whippings and fines were meted out as punishment for profanity, fornication, traveling on Sunday, and theft. If you were one of those who failed to attend church services on a regular basis, you were fined heavily. Twenty lashes were ordered for John Evans in 1785 for questioning the veracity of the Scriptures. In the years of Revolution, the courthouse shifted to supporting the law as benefited the rebellious colonists.

Then there were the odd arrangements of New England law. So-called "shift marriages" were entered into here as they were in other northeast precincts. A widow could remarry without carrying her deceased husband's debts with her if she stood up in nothing but her shift. This was Massachusetts law as exported to the Territory of Maine. There were many married not only in their shifts, but also astride the boundary lines of intersecting counties, to avoid being subject to the jurisdiction of certain courts.

The Lincoln County Historical Society purchased the courthouse from the descendants of Major Samuel Goodwin in 1954. As I idle about the grounds taking pictures, a historical society member offers me a tour. I step inside while *Merlin* waits. I find that the flavor of the old place has been well kept: original timbers and pine planks, some of the latter as wide as fifty-two inches, are exposed, and the courtroom seems surprisingly elegant for a country place. The air is cool, smelling of very old unfinished wood and hundreds of years of human presence. In the eaves, the tarry smell of the sun-warmed old roof permeates the air, and aged spinning wheels and looms gather dust. The ancient beehive oven fireplace presides in the tavern kitchen.

While the meeting of sessions was eventually moved to Wiscasset, the building remains as a monument to the earliest days of civil structure in Lincoln County. It is still possible today to sit quietly in one of these rooms and, if you have imagination enough, to hear the absent British-scented talk of yesterday—the droning of courtroom procedure and legal argument—and to feel the faded warmth of tavern fires in this timeless structure on Courthouse Point.

MERLIN AND I embark southward once again on the last water we will cover today. The river shows signs of settlement now, both colonial and modern. Here and there, houses nearly as old as the courthouse are mixed with those built in the present. In another quarter hour, the Richmond bridge comes into sight as I ride the slack current toward this wide, five-span structure. We pass a cove to the east, moving closer to inspect. The current sometimes keeps patches of open water here from sealing themselves with seasonal ice. I have watched bald eagles fish this spot in midwinter when other favorite areas are iced over.

In the season of cold, the Richmond bridge collects crumbling sheet ice like Wall Street bankers collect gold. An unseasonable breakup in December 2003 piled blocks of river ice against support pilings nearly to the bridge deck. Sometimes the rubble contains worrisome chunks of substantial size; occasionally the ice bunches up in innumerable stacks of what appear to be pieces of broken china destroyed in a magnificent tantrum. Ice of this size and density acts as an efficient barrier to downriver discharge and can back up water over the banks in communities upriver. More typically, breakup happens anywhere from late February to late March, though the actual moment is ever unpredictable. People along the river wish for an early spring season of slow, measured warming lest both ice and runoff gallop south together.

Beyond this ice-catcher of a bridge, the Kennebec abruptly divides into a broad, Y-shaped bay. The narrower channel bears to the right and the village of Richmond, while the main, leftward channel continues south. Between the two lies the considerable bulk of Swan Island, the east shore of which I will visit

The Kennebec at Richmond Bridge

tomorrow. If a quick freeze occurs during winter, sometimes the current here is captured in a frozen arc of ice that curves toward the main (east) channel, rather like water leaving a raised footprint.

For now, *Merlin* and I cruise the last half mile of the westerly channel toward town. Passing the state landing on Swan's west side, we pick our way among a small collection of powerboats and sailing craft in Richmond's sheltered little harbor. *Merlin* transcribes a small arc as we come ashore at a gravel ramp in the shadow of the town's old brick mill buildings. Richmond is a place of fine, old mansions and smaller, newer homes; its tiny downtown is being discovered, old buildings being converted to new uses. Richmond has a certain fame as the place where the White Russians live, given that it is the scene of a small Russian transplantation beginning in the 1920s. There are two Orthodox churches here. Willis Johnson's superb book, *The Girl Who Would Be Russian,* is an award-winning testament to this unusual migratory accident.

Walking on solid ground has a certain novel feeling. I have piloted *Merlin* over twenty miles this day, more than forty today and yesterday combined, nearly eighty miles in four days if I include my digressions on the St. George. Tomorrow I will cover a shorter point-to-point route to Merrymeeting Bay, but I will add extra miles in what I hope will be a successful digression up the Eastern River. From there I will drift south to the bay and then up the lower stretch of the Cathance.

Merlin has served so well that I've felt only agreeably tired each night after many hours spent on this Thoreauesque escape, and so it is today. I have no sore muscles or any of the other debilities people complain about when going for distance in this kind of boat. (Kayaker Web sites are full of interminable discussion about the Holy Grail of comfortable seating.) I will get a workout during my final days on these rivers. Given how well the journey has gone to here, I feel confident about undertaking the more demanding water I will see in the next couple of days. Still, as I load *Merlin* onto a neighbor's car, I think ahead to the last day of my travels, when I will try to navigate the Back River to the unpredictable and powerful waters of the lower Kennebec all the way to the Atlantic.

Day Six

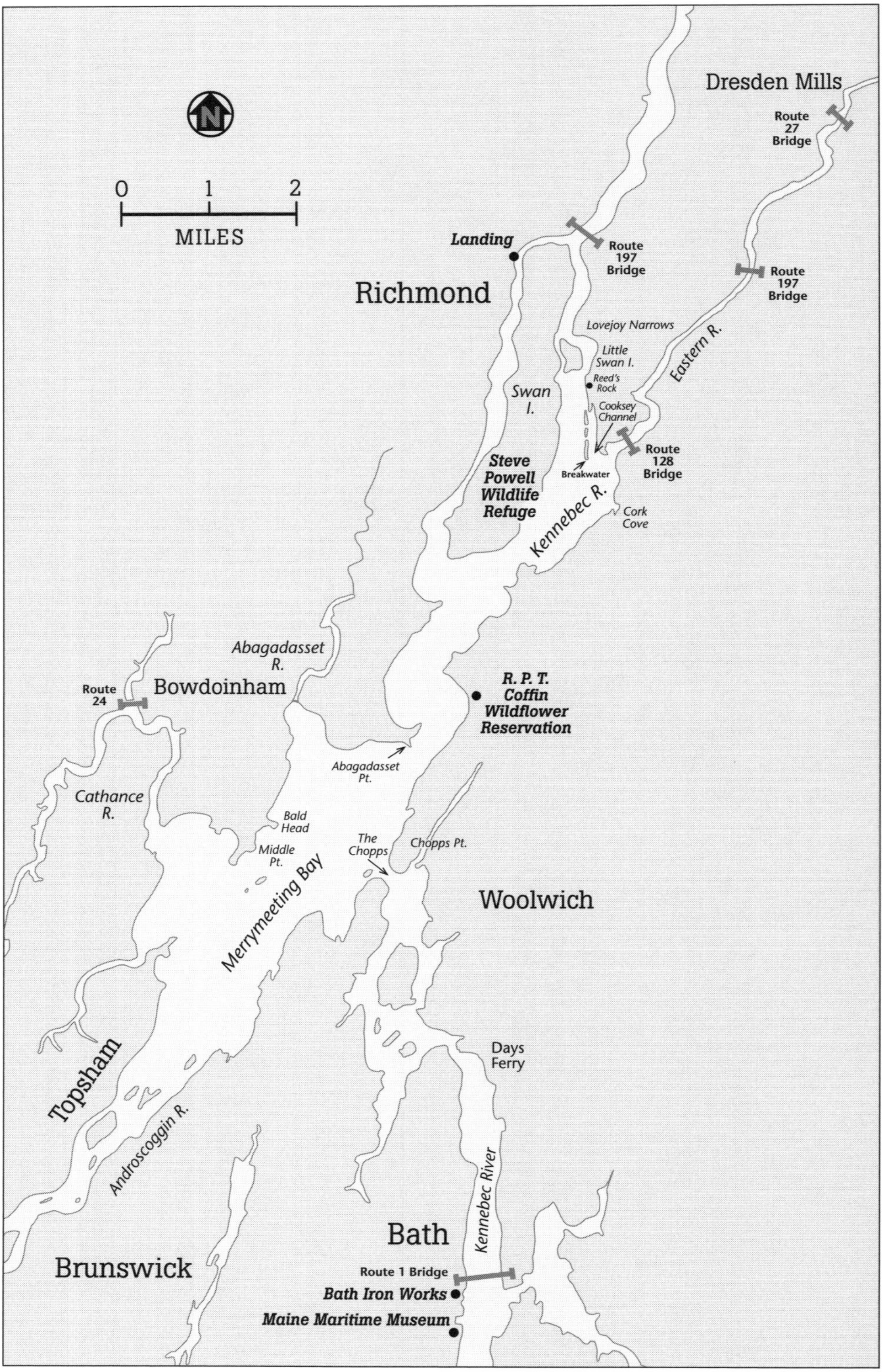

Dresden Mills
Route 27 Bridge
N
0 1 2
MILES
Landing
Route 197 Bridge
Route 197 Bridge
Richmond
Lovejoy Narrows
Little Swan I.
Eastern R.
Reed's Rock
Swan I.
Cooksey Channel
Route 128 Bridge
Steve Powell Wildlife Refuge
Breakwater
Kennebec R.
Cork Cove
Abagadasset R.
Route 24
Bowdoinham
R. P. T. Coffin Wildflower Reservation
Abagadasset Pt.
Cathance R.
Bald Head
Middle Pt.
The Chopps
Chopps Pt.
Merrymeeting Bay
Woolwich
Days Ferry
Topsham
Androscoggin R.
Kennebec River
Bath
Brunswick
Route 1 Bridge
Bath Iron Works
Maine Maritime Museum

The Kennebec, Eastern, and Cathance

[T]he green world in much of Maine has been turned upside down. . . . With these losses comes further change. . . . While observers may be inclined to mourn the loss of forest trees as I mourn the loss of part of my apple tree, the forest they miss looked the way it did only because of past disturbance.

—Kent Ryden

Landscape with Figures: Nature and Culture in New England (2001)

Excellent weather this morning. I arrive back at Richmond early on my sixth day out. The village is about as quiet as a crossroads can get. Jay Harper and his son Devin are unloading their boats at the harbor ramp and getting ready to join me for a paddle downriver. Jay and I have been planning to explore parts of the Kennebec together for some time. It seems a good idea to meld that outing with my need to press downstream to Merrymeeting Bay today with perhaps an exploration of the Eastern River toward Dresden. Then there is the matter of a short end-of-day diversion up the Cathance to Bowdoinham. Jay and Devin will meet me there at the end of the day. In the meantime, it will be good to have two accomplices in my watery meanderings and to carry along potential rescuers if I do something especially clumsy.

Our little flotilla heads north out of unruffled Richmond Harbor, around the north end of big Swan Island and into the Kennebec's main current. A lone green buoy tilts in the lanes beyond the Foster Preserve dock. I can feel the downward push of the river here. We will have a comfortable ride down Swan's east shore, and proceed to steer the boats in that direction, each of us taking turns in the lead. A muddle of ledge surrounds the northern tip of Swan and, above, old houses dating from the days of earliest settlement here still stand in trimmed fields. The river makes a broad basin with dense woodlands along its east limits opposite the island. Other than the structures on Swan, no houses intrude as the river narrows some and shifts direction. Though mainly thickly wooded, this section of the island reveals occasional open ground surrounded by towering white pines.

We continue southwest in single file, each keeping track of the other, and approach another point of divergence in the Kennebec where the main river stays left and a narrower channel bears right, hugging Swan's shoreline. Little Swan Island separates the two waterways. Like some whiskered sentinel, a huge, granite glacial erratic topped with a cluster of lichen-strewn jack pines marks the point of separation. One can go around either side of the whaleback, and I tuck in behind it, emerging in the smaller channel feeling the tug of current on *Merlin*'s stern in several directions. This is a wild looking junction, no buildings, markers, or other signs of human presence, just rock and flowing water, and that suits fine.

Devin and Jay take the lead and I follow as we begin the unusual experience of making our way south on this sheltered, primeval stream between the two islands. It is quieter here than on the main channel. The glint of warm sun on the water in this attractive, hidden passage beckons us southward. Our procession gets broken up as each of us stops periodically to take in the extraordinary attractiveness of this place. Watermarks—grey, black, and horizontal—stain the granite ledge that lines the passage. Red spruce, hemlock, white pine, red oak, and birch crowd down to the shore. Devin pauses a moment and sits on a bar of ledge under low hemlock branches to wait for us, contentedly sampling the densely wooded shore.

Another few minutes of this slow, serene proceeding and we come to the state-operated campground that is at the center of the island. In summer, you can paddle to the Stephen Foster Preserve under your own steam, or arrive via a state launch that makes several trips daily to the mainland at Richmond from the island's other side. A few campers are setting up tents, and there is the smell of a campfire. We wave and then bear first to the east, as the channel bends and twists its way around more high ledge, and then southward. A quintessential Maine landscape.

The current provides a gentle assist as we pass hemlock cover that becomes a perfect foil, its green and darker under-green a contrast to the yellow sunlight. Drifting along, the gentlest stroke is adequate to send us forward in this easy stream. No powerboats burn by to interrupt this splendid interlude. Soon we near the lower end of the back channel, emerge, and turn east in dozens of acres of tall, waving *Spartina*, its green expanse trending off to the south as far as we can see.

ONE OF THE GREAT Kennebec legends is that of Jacataqua, an Indian queen, who resided on Swan Island and who became the bride of a Revolutionary soldier. This queen of mixed French and Abenaki blood was fabled to run the Kennebec shores with an English bloodhound. No ordinary fellow, her husband was the ambitious and traitorous Aaron Burr, who saw preferment for himself in joining Arnold's march to Quebec. Burr was a complex and contradictory man whom Bowdoin's Robert P. Tristram Coffin called "the Judas Iscariot of American history." When Burr attempted to kill a marauding bear that had been devastating local crops, Jacataqua saved him from what promised to be a fatal mauling. The bear and her cubs, shot by Jacataqua, became the center of a feast for the riverside community of Cushnoc.

Jacataqua and her dog stayed with Burr on the bitter journey to Quebec, where she gave birth to their daughter. Coffin, in his *Kennebec: Cradle of Americans*, extends the tale by suggesting that Burr might have brought his tawny queen to Long Island, New York, where they maintained their relationship secretly for years. She was said to have drowned herself upon hearing that her husband had shot Alexander Hamilton.

WE COME UPON three people in a skiff who have just come off the main river and are fishing the edges of the marsh. No one seems to steer the sputtering boat, and the two men are, in any case, preoccupied with the tangle of fishing lines in which they have wrapped themselves. Their little dog barks and snarls viciously at us while an older woman in the boat ignores the dog's yelping and smokes furiously. We say hello, but no one responds. Ah, signs of a modern presence. I have spoken too soon about powerboats, for, in addition to our friends with the swell dog, two large, high, bulbous cabin cruisers hurtle down the Kennebec in front of us where the channels join. At speed, they throw an enormous wake behind them, which we brace to take head on.

We're bound for the other side of the river and need to press on. I sight on a small cabin in the woods on the far side of the Kennebec's main channel near Reed's Rock, set *Merlin*'s bow for that destination, and paddle like hell. The feeling is rather like trying to cross the six lanes of the Van Wyck Expressway in Queens on foot during rush hour. Luckily, I have adequate time to find a place for myself in the shallows on the Kennebec's east side before another overlarge craft comes thumping along, sending big waves into the weeds. Jay and Devin await their chance and then come hastily across. I had forgotten that today is Saturday. It's the weekend! I suspect a whole legion of Walter Mittys will shortly come lumbering down this fine river, eager to discharge the angst of a week behind a desk or similar. Of course, you do that by throttling up. Show the river who's boss. Beat it up. Right. The change from that marvelous quiet I have been enjoying all week is uncomfortably obvious.

A FEW DAYS BACK, I spoke with Naomi Schalit, director of Maine Rivers, a citizens' organization that represents a variety of river rehabilitation and preservation efforts across Maine. I wanted to get a wider perspective on the health of moving water in the state and to think aloud with someone who follows the river scene on a daily basis. She is a compact, intelligent woman driven by an energetic sense of how one of Maine's greatest resources might be used better. We talked in her Augusta office.

I shared with her my enthusiasm over the improvement I saw in the rivers I had scouted. They were cleaner by far than they had been a few decades ago, when in certain communities one could smell the larger rivers even before laying eyes on them. Schalit confirmed that a lot of progress has been made. The rivers are healthier than they have been in a long while, we agreed. However, the picture is far from perfect.

"There's a danger in the success of the Clean Water Act," she told me. "People may get complacent and think there are no further dangers to these rivers. We've moved from restraining the biggest polluters, who were obvious, to a situation of death by a thousand cuts." Obvious sources of pollution have given way, in part, to many smaller sources: hidden discharge pipes, overflowing sewage entering rivers, and other non–point-source pollution.

Schalit and her organization plan to raise public awareness of the value of Maine rivers and to promote river restoration. "It isn't enough to say we've cleaned up a river," Schalit observed. "We need to *restore* rivers; we need more birds, aquatic animals, prey species, and everything else that goes with healthy rivers. We need more public support for river restoration."

Even with relative success in slowing down the dumping of pollutants in these waters, Schalit emphasized that there are new problems. Who has a right to take large amounts of water from important rivers, and how much? When not only paper mills but also ski areas or golf courses drain large amounts of water from a river, fish and a whole range of aquatic and avian species dependent on them are affected or even killed. Most permitting standards for drawing water in these quantities or for discharging effluent are out of date and heavily influenced by those who use water in manufacturing. Schalit pointed particularly to the paper industry, which she believes has "held sway in the Maine legislature way out of proportion to what should have been allowed."

"Healthy rivers in Maine can be a major source of economic growth," she acknowledged, "but the polluters get listened to more in the legislature. People need to get politically active. There's a lack of awareness of the subtle issues that threaten rivers. Lakes, rivers, marshes, the entire marine environment—are all connected," she said. "They affect all of us."

MAKING OUR WAY easily down the east shallows, with interesting views back across the river to Swan Island, we soon encounter a long, raised berm that stretches downriver below Reed's Rock. I set about searching for the entry to the Eastern River, which lies somewhere behind all this gravel and weed. It is shallow and sandy here, and we stroke several hundred yards south before finding a cut in the berm and then slide through. We are tempted to turn north in the Cooksey Channel, where there seems to be a narrow corridor amongst high cattails, though after a little exploration this way begins to look doubtful, and much speculative discussion follows. What if we get way up in there and find only a muddy dead end? I put on my explorer's hat, looking as much like Sir Francis Drake as possible, and order Jay and Devin to follow me in the opposite direction.

The chart shows the river mouth south of here, and south we paddle. Well, not exactly. Jay observes that none of us has eaten anything substantial since early morning and that Devin is looking a bit faint. Come to think of it, my blood sugar has languished a bit, too. OK. Putting ashore on the gravel bar that separates us now from the main channel, we commence to open the hatches and rummage about. Out come the water bottles and sandwiches, a little obeisance to dehydration and hunger. We all admire a red-berried, low-bush shrub that seems to want to take over this berm, but we can't identify it. The sun brings pleasant warmth, and a certain temptation regarding naps invades my bones, as usual. I always find it comforting to be tired for the right reasons.

Time moves, lunch is finished, and we continue south in this weedy back channel. I haven't gone far when something large and sturgeonlike hits *Merlin*'s keel and then moves off quickly, leaving behind an explosion of disturbed river bottom. First time *Merlin* and I have been whacked by a surprised big fish. The sturgeon is present in these waters, in this very neighborhood, in fact, and the subject of concern about preservation. Next to the coelacanth, the sturgeon appears to me our best living relic of prehistoric river bottoms, looking rather like a moody carp crossed with a broken chain saw all covered with armor plate. I shall wonder for a long time if a sturgeon was the creature that threw a punch at *Merlin*'s hull.

The Cooksey Channel has a maximum depth of twenty feet but is a good deal shallower in most places. Cutting across the stubble in depths of two and three feet, I finally locate the entrance to the Eastern. Off to my left is the great wavering marsh, Middle Ground. Jay and Devin will head back to Richmond from here and pick up the car. We will rendezvous later in Bowdoinham. While I bear east and north up the Eastern, they head out beyond the tidal wall and turn north. Both are paddling full tilt, dealing side-on with the Kennebec's pushy current. The breeze is now rolling up channel.

I will pick up more of the Kennebec shortly, but for now, I have in mind sampling this intriguing smaller river. My hope is to ride up the Eastern a ways toward Dresden Mills, which I have seen little bits of from land but never from the water. Then I'll dash down to the entrance of the Cathance through Merrymeeting Bay on the slack and wrap up the day by following the Cathance to Bowdoinham. All this may be overly ambitious, but I shall try.

THE EASTERN curves northeast and east, perhaps accounting for its name. A pretty, secluded river, it connects the Kennebec with a few crossroads villages upstream. Its course meanders generally northeastward for more than twenty miles into rural backcountry, but today I want only to cover the water between the Kennebec and the Maine Route 27 bridge at Dresden. I skirt the marsh, working my way upriver, passing Webb's Point and Cork Cove. In January, Middle Ground marsh is buried in ice, and a whole colony of fish shacks appears, each perched over the Eastern's current.

The marsh waves densely green as I turn, make my way past a brick-red Colonial farmhouse, and duck under the Route 128 bridge. The Eastern pulls more to the north now. Great fields lie above the banking to my left; there are large family farms here that yield heavenly strawberries, corn, and vegetables. I wave to someone on a tractor in a back field. The flatness of this triangle of land between the Kennebec and Eastern must be due to the two rivers occasionally washing over this surface during rare times of flooding, a fate that no doubt contributes to the land's fertility.

The Eastern ascends in a series of steps, first north and then east. The river soon bends and inches its way under a very old, latticed steel arch in a cleft between two high banks. It then makes its way through a series of gentle meanders, first north and then again to a bearing of eighty degrees. My little side trip is effortless, the current moderate and the wind absent. The fields give way to dense white pines and brush. Here and there small pastures are going back to woods.

Dipping the paddle steadily, I attempt to see as much as I can of the river

Eastern River, Dresden Mills

in an hour and a half. *Merlin* completes another north-then-east latch step, and we are in a broad bend heading nearly eastward. This is the style of river I like—gently turning now and then, and about twenty-five yards across. Something intimate asserts itself here. Scattered houses and old barns appear now and then as *Merlin* slides along. Tilting at various angles along the shore, more ice-fishing shacks look very out of season. Thoughts of ice remind me of how brief the fine days of summer are in Maine. A cost is exacted for the privilege of trending up these rivers, and it is paid in the early arrival of ice and snow. For now, we are still in the last hours of summer.

I think of such farms, fields, and woods as typical of many parts of Maine 150 years ago; each crossroad a little center of civility in a northern, inhospitable country. The people who lived in Maine's remoteness, and some were my ancestors, were possessed of a hardiness and resolve that is increasingly rare today. They were usually plain people without pretense, and that ethic still survives along these rivers. I am not alone in thinking they were, in a small way back then, heroes.

Ralph Waldo Emerson, Thoreau's friend and sometime mentor and neighbor, was, like Thoreau, ever in search of the natural man. In the fall of 1849, he began an essay, never published, about an Indian of whom he had learned from Thoreau's Maine stories. Alec Therrien interested Emerson because he embodied a kind of woodsy heroism that Emerson thought he had not written about enough.

Modern biographers have suggested that, as he edited the final text of *Representative Men*, Emerson believed he had somehow neglected "average" working people who embodied a heroism in the rough lives they lived as river men, small frontier farmers, woodsmen, craftsmen, and, yes, ice men. Even as he prepared his manuscript on the habits of the great, Emerson understood that country fellows like Therrien, of Indian and Quebecois blood, were more embedded in the natural world, closer to the earth, and better for it, than the famous whom he chronicled.

Emerson came to Maine a number of times, but he did not write about it as did Thoreau. Nonetheless, Maine lodged in his mind, thanks to the recounting Thoreau gave him, and Emerson saw it as home to the natural or spiritual man. "The brave Therrien stands well as Adam did, as an Indian does, as a lion or a bull or one of Homer's heroes," wrote Emerson. Those who relied on their own skill in remote places and who daily remained close to natural influences, thought Emerson, were privy to some kind of universal truth that most men of the city could not obtain.

One of the nice things about the Eastern, I discover, is its motor-free serenity. Several guidebooks describe this as a quiet getaway, and their descriptions are correct. Dense brush and lines of trees bend to the river. Taken-over fields lay beyond to the north. In another quarter-hour, I round the bend at Dresden Mills, and the Route 27 bridge hovers in sight. Ducks and geese quack and play in a farm pond across the road. From what I have gleaned from histories of the industry, icehouses once sat along the banks somewhere along here, not as numerous as on the Kennebec, but a part of that transformation created by the frozen-water industry nonetheless. I see no remnants above the riverbanks. How rapidly a whole way of life slips away.

Turning in the pool west of the bridge, *Merlin* and I idle in the easy current, just looking around. I have seen many bald eagles here in winter. A farm nearby used to throw offal on the ice when slaughtering or during lambing, and eagles, mature and immature, would feed here when the ice rendered it impossible for them to fish. A cormorant is the only large bird working these waters now, and he seems unruffled by my presence. An old truck makes its way slowly north on Route 27 as the day winds down. No other sound breaks the afternoon. Without further ceremony, *Merlin* and I dig in, making southwest for the Kennebec again.

EXITING THE EASTERN, glad to have seen little corners of its private self, I know I will explore it upriver when I have more time. Now, back on the Kennebec, my task is to negotiate the current downriver to Merrymeeting Bay in a timely and undramatic way. My interim destination, though several miles away, is nearly in sight; the turn to the Cathance opens on the west side of the bay not far beyond Abagadasset Point. I will need to work the river to the southwest as it widens into what some have labeled the largest bay north of the Chesapeake.

The Friends of Merrymeeting Bay calculate that the catchment here runs to something like nine thousand acres. The Androscoggin, Cathance, and Kennebec all collide in this bay, each charged with their normal tidal complement, runoff from half the state west and north of here, and whatever ice or rain might be arriving in the present. The bay also takes in the waters of the more modest Abagadasset and Muddy rivers, the latter flowing east from Topsham. The Friends group calls this bay an inland delta with ties to the Kennebec River estuary. Salmon, river herring, shad, smelt, striped bass, and exotic species such as short-nosed and Atlantic sturgeon live or spawn here. The Nature Conservancy says about 20 percent of Maine's tidal marshes bloom in this area and fifty species of freshwater fish move about in the bay. It's a major ecological crossroads. The lower Kennebec is Merrymeeting Bay's only outlet.

These can be problematic waters for a kayaker, with the current working in multiple directions and a fair amount of big boat traffic. Certain spots farther down beyond the Chopps, are challenging when the tide is running. The river turns eastward not far above Bath and becomes an island-strewn pool just north of Days Ferry. There, all the water the bay has collected gets pushed through the narrow bend at Thorne Head. Compression means acceleration, countercurrents, powerful and deceptive eddies, and whatever other forms of mischief rivers can get up to. I will not get below the Chopps today, and the water in front of me looks serene enough, so I make my way southward feeling reassured.

A few miles below the bottom of Merrymeeting, still another river, the Sasanoa, enters the Kennebec from the east, opposite Bath, bringing its own restlessness with it. The tide there may run in either direction and not necessarily in synchrony with the Kennebec's movement. I will ride east of the Sasanoa on another day, avoiding its two perverse reversing falls, picking my way along the Back River to join the lower Kennebec about eight miles below Bath and Woolwich.

AFTER BEING on the water for several days, one begins to notice a change in the anchors of everyday, composed life, and that sticks with me now. The sense of being lodged in a fluid world takes over. The paddler goes to bed and checks the initial and secondary stability of the cot, feeling on entry that one is not secure in paddling position. The cot seems to rock a little even if nailed to the floor. Television appears even more revolting than usual. One sneaks about in late evenings, checking paddles, life jacket, food for tomorrow, and other necessaries. A certain looking forward to dawn persists. People wonder what you are doing these days even after you have told them. It is hard to fathom, after all—this spending more time on the water than on the couch.

The full force of these changes is felt, of course, in the boat. Points of reference are altered beyond expectation. Time matters only in its relation to tides. Hunger goes unnoticed. The grim fascination of bill payments dissolves. Commuting, as millions live it, seems the ultimate absurdity. Politics equally so.

As you follow the current, new markers become relevant, important. The behavior of moving water in its many, many permutations becomes something read often. It is, you remember, the very bed on which you have deigned to lie. The shore, rich with the character of place, offers a linear series of indicators as to where you are on the river and in the world. Buoys appear occasionally to announce ledge and position in the currents. Sometimes buildings with an unmistakable signature, or a known bridge, or an island mark your progress. The position of the sun draws attention, as do its shadows. A few people, working here and there on the stream, act as reminders of a careful human use of the water. All of these signs and others replace the commonplace as objects of interest.

You also attune to the boat itself and its unique character. How the paddle is held, the efficiency of the stroke. The slightest lean of the hull and how the boat is trimmed. How you sit in the cockpit. The manner in which wind and wave are taken over the bow. The feel of the boat as it moves through varying situations. What you can risk and what you cannot.

If these conditions are reckoned carefully, the journey assembles like clockwork—smoothly, with all desired speed. When you get it right, there are few finer moments, the kayak sliding forward briskly, your direction taking advantage of current and wind, water covered efficiently and—most important—the whole thing so conveniently orchestrated that you can detach and breathe in the air, shore, sun-soaked drift of the water's surface, and the different world each new minute presents.

I DECIDE to follow the Kennebec farther along its east side. Coming down that way, I postpone making the crossover until I am more into the bay at a point where I expect that crosscurrents will not be a problem. As *Merlin* bores downstream in the Kennebec's main channel, I feel only a slight nudge from the tide and figure I will manage a relatively easy trip to the Cathance. I pull away from the south end of Swan and the great, green marsh to its south known simply as the Swan Island flats. These acres of river mud are exposed at low water and are backed by dense tangles of brush and hardwoods. I make good time along the shore as the river widens to become bay. Ducks and gulls are airborne as I slide nearer the point where the river becomes salt. About two miles below the mouth of the Eastern a high-tension power line angles across the bay at Abagadasset Point, and here it occurs to me that I am only minutes above some attractive wild land on the east bank where it might be good to pause.

The New England Wildflower Society has preserved the Robert P. T. Coffin Wildflower Sanctuary on the Kennebec's east bank above Chopps Point. Keeping to the left of the main current, I paddle slowly in search of landmarks. The preserve isn't signed, so I look for a sizable piece of flat ledge sheltered by an old oak that dips nearly to the water's surface. It isn't hard to find at the south end of grassy Lilly Cove. *Merlin* rides on a tether while I climb the bank and walk the trail uphill. After four hours in the saddle, my legs demand some stretching. I not only get a chance to work out the kinks here, but the woods are strikingly pretty, dotted with a variety of wildflower species in season. At the center of the tract, a grove of Atlantic white cedar grows beside the trail.

Approachable by land or water, the preserve is peaceful woodland and not much visited. It is a welcoming place to ruminate on a summer or autumn afternoon. An hour or two can be spent here just tramping about, identifying

Kennebec River, looking south to Merrymeeting Bay

plants and enjoying the river view. I say hello to two elderly ladies who are walking the trails, obviously possessors of that higher knowledge that only a lifetime of discerning plant fancy can convey. After twenty minutes of roaming around and doing deep knee bends, like some stick insect that has just discovered it has legs, I crawl aboard *Merlin* again. Recrossing the river, I turn south, certain I now hold the record for back and forth Kennebec river crossings in one day.

Merrymeeting Bay, combining the full force of both the Kennebec and the Androscoggin, is a guess-what's-coming-for-dinner neighborhood. Move in one direction, and you are coping with the tidal inflow. Move in another direction, and the Androscoggin may want to push you east. Get in the middle of the main channel of the Kennebec when the tide is on its way out, and you may get a quicker-than-planned-for ride through the Chopps. I paddle rapidly to get myself out of the push-pull of the main channel. My ears are cocked and my eyes open to watch for powerboats hurrying up or down river. The lower reaches of this broad catchment are also just above the point where the tongue of inbound Kennebec tidal currents dives and is overridden by the warmer waters coming downstream from the rivers, producing a layered effect and sometimes a further confusion of movement. I avoid the worst of all this by working my way to the west.

Merlin rides easily as we make steady progress downwind along the western shore, staying with the shallow, protected flats that verge on the bay's enormous marsh area. My real work now is to find the entrance to the Cathance River. Calculating that less than an hour on the smaller river will get me to Bowdoinham, where I expect to meet Jay and Devin, I ease along looking for landmarks. Dead ahead opens the mouth of the Androscoggin, the river trading water with the Kennebec in this vast watery basin. To the south, beyond the Chopps and Days Ferry, is Bath, a fine little city, the tops of whose highest structures drop in and out of view as I paddle. It's a community with a history deeply tied to the Kennebec.

IN THE DISTANCE, at the city's core, lies Bath Iron Works, a major fixture on this river for over a century and heir to long-disappeared centers of large shipbuilding farther down east. If Damariscotta and Wiscasset enjoyed a certain heyday as Maine shipbuilding hubs, the latter-day mecca of the region is Bath. The two smaller communities yielded their shipbuilding dominance slowly in the 1800s.

One might argue that Bath rose to prominence as a shipbuilding nexus largely through the efforts of one family. Lebanon, Connecticut, native Jonathon Hyde arrived in Maine searching for work in 1792. He built a general store and ships' chandlery on Water Street and soon did business in shipbuilding, banking, and insurance. Hyde's brother, Zina, had a son, Thomas, who attended Bowdoin College and then served in the Union Army. He became a brigadier general by the age of twenty-three, an indicator of his notable gift for successfully marshalling people and resources.

Coming home, Thomas Hyde took over a small local iron foundry in Bath. He ignited the business of shipbuilding on the lower Kennebec, became one of Maine's most influential industrialists, the mayor of Bath, and, in 1874, Maine Senate president. His great contribution to shipbuilding along these waters, besides his organizing genius, was his foresight in recognizing that the coming era would be one of steel, not wooden, ships. He brought his holdings together as Bath Iron Works in 1884. Soon thereafter, his company absorbed marine engine builder Gross Marine Iron Works. The *Cottage City* and the *Manhattan* were the first two (wooden) ships constructed under the roof of the newly formed Bath Iron Works, followed by the *Machias* and *Castine*, the yard's first two orders for the U.S. Navy.

When the Hyde family first knew Bath, the city was not much more than a collection of houses and wharves, a rough place of log forts and local commerce. Garnett Laidlaw Eskew, in *Cradle of Ships*, describes the lower reaches of this river in their pristine state, as young Thomas Hyde must have first seen them. What Hyde found on his return from Civil War battlefields was a settlement still wooded and rural in nature, with most of its activity centered on the waterfront. It was a town all right, but a small one, yet to achieve its place in the world. The banks of the Kennebec were heavily wooded, as were river and offshore islands such as Seguin. Bath was a riverside nest of potential, and young Hyde would see it as such, making it a shipbuilding powerhouse.

Anyone crossing the Bath bridge today by the present Bath Iron Works will see the hulls and superstructure of two Aegis guided-missile destroyers riding at anchor, undergoing further fitting out. (Thomas Hyde's prodigy is one of only two facilities in America building the Aegis warships.) The Bath skyline rises in silhouette to the west: on one end, churches and distinguished old Federal-style buildings, and on the other, a cluster of cranes, industrial shops, and launch facilities cheek by jowl with the Maine Maritime Museum.

MERLIN EDGES SOUTHWESTWARD. Feeling a strengthening breeze coming upriver, and with the sun in my eyes, I look for three distinct headlands to my right. One by one, I pass Bald Head, Middle Point, and Center Point. With Brick Island to my left, I make the turn, pointing *Merlin* into a pleasant avenue of water trending northwest. At its uppermost end lies the entrance to the Cathance and my route to nearby Bowdoinham.

The Cathance's mouth is a somewhat narrow and occasionally shallow channel southwest of Beach Point. It's a good river to paddle when the tide is building or full. I progress north slowly through wooded countryside as maneuvering room grows scarce. The river seems quiet, even private, as it gradually bends north-northeast and then more northerly again as *Merlin* and I push upstream. Gulls circle and drift behind me toward Merrymeeting. The Cathance eventually assumes the shape of a broad Y, its nexus at the village of Bowdoinham and its two arms meandering some distance off into the backcountry. The right arm connects with a marshy region north of the town, while the left arm plunges south and then west, becoming eventually too shallow for navigation as it wends its way through farmlands.

Passing a boggy zone to my right, I paddle through a broad S-curve about twenty minutes in from the bay and soon find the junction where the Cathance divides. Pretty little Bowdoinham lies before me, and upriver a few hundred yards I come to the town landing. This is as far as I will explore today. Jay and Devin are waiting. We pull *Merlin* from the water and are soon on the highway headed northward. As we trend toward home, I add the Cathance to that growing list of rivers I will travel further. It is an ideal waterway for casual poking into upstream nooks and crannies.

Day Seven

THE CATHANCE AGAIN

Shortly after Glous'gap came here, he fashioned a shelter for himself . . . the Creator Kesoulk then found work for him to do: "With your wooden bow carve all the brooks, streams and rivers. . . . Make each deep and clean so these waters run clear and quick to the ocean." So Glous'gap began carving and cleaning all the waterways of the land, forming the riverbottoms that carried these waters to the endless salt sea to eastward.

—Based on the "The Coming of Glous'gap"
as retold by Michael Runningwolf and Patricia Clark Smith
in *On the Trail of Elder Brother: Glous'gap Stories of the MicMac Indians,* 2000

Last night I sat at home, planning my final day on the big rivers. It wasn't long, consulting my tide charts, before I realized that today wasn't going to be the ideal moment for the long paddle from Wiscasset to the Kennebec's mouth at Popham. The full tide comes either much too early or rather too late. I have to delay for a day and start my run on the final portion of the Kennebec early tomorrow. As the evening wore on, I thought about how pleasant yesterday's climb from Merrymeeting Bay to Bowdoinham had been, and decided to go back and spend today exploring the upper Cathance as far as the stream will allow. A busman's holiday.

As the morning arrives the weather looks favorable. I prepare *Merlin* for my unplanned upriver outing in Bowdoinham. After finishing my notes from yesterday, I motor south, spying on the Kennebec as we go. It is early afternoon by the time I arrive. The Cathance has begun filling quietly, a handful of power boats ride at their moorings, and I hear the voices of several people who are making ready for an afternoon's outing beyond Merrymeeting Bay. Ready to launch, I carry *Merlin* down the ramp and we are off, turning southwest under the iron bridge.

The river here is broad, making a wide bend to the south. Waving fields of marsh grass, scrub, and thick, riotous water plants flank the channel on both left and right. I am alone on the water as I head inland, the river charting broad, sweeping bends along muddy shelves backed by shoulder-tall cordgrass. Wide, uncluttered, and open, the sky seems limitless. A cluster of dark nimbus—or should I say nimbi?—rides on the western horizon. I see animal tracks of all sorts in the mud. An osprey swoops low and observes my progress.

In less than a mile, the Cathance forms a broad dog's leg to the west, and *Merlin* rides easily along a row of sinewy trees that border the river edge. Marsh vegetation grows tall here too. Soon the channel is walled in to east and west, but the open river is so broad that I'm able to gaze above the marsh to dense woodlands well back. The Cathance is a meandering river that has carved a continuing series of opposed half-moon bends. Several ice shacks decked out in bright hues hold their rusty chimneys above the waving green along the forest border. An osprey circles overhead and prepares to stoop. For a moment it seems I am the target, but he veers away and sweeps the water just to my left. I push southward, the river's surface surprisingly glasslike, the direction of the channel pulling first southeast and then southwest.

I stroke closer to the line of woods that borders the marsh to my right as a bald eagle comes upriver rapidly, skimming only a few feet above the river's surface. At first it looks like another osprey, but as it passes I see its distinctive eagle markings and size. I have seen eagles fairly often during these days on the water, their presence telling of a reassuring comeback from near elimination in this region, but I have never before seen *Haliaeetus leucocephalus* skimming barely above the surface like this. I am absolutely charmed by this interesting place, which I have quite to myself. The Cathance is, I find, an intimate river of great privacy, stillness, and solitude.

Entrances to side channels go by, little islands come and go. The river winds under a powerline, skirts an island and back channel, and then narrows.

Boat launch site at Bowdoinham, on the Cathance River

It's shallower here; I am not much above the marsh weed I see on the river-bottom. I point *Merlin* to where the channel runs deeper, and we round another bend to the southwest. It feels even wilder now, the woods pressing in from either side, the marsh in a tangle to my left. Out of the corner of my eye I see something move on the shore, and a muskrat saunters out from the brush and into the stream, disappearing quickly, soundlessly, under my boat as I pass.

The Cathance pulls rightward. I pass a little elongated island, an eyeot, and the river becomes suddenly a mere thread. Ahead, a shape remains motionless, and as I get closer, letting *Merlin* drift silently, I spot an immature bald eagle perched on a stump in the stream. He sits still, watching for whatever the river might provide. I guess he is about two years old, still in the last days of his youthful coat and beginning to put on the feathers of an adult. Moving not a muscle, I continue to drift, and the large bird allows us to pass within fifteen feet without taking flight. We stare at each other, and then he is behind me. Another minute, and I hear the flap of his substantial wings, a whooshing sound like wheat being threshed. As they say, this certainly beats sitting in the office.

As I paddle on, the river loses more depth and makes another half loop southeast. A rocky abutment comes unexpectedly into view, and, above it, an old railroad bridge spans the river. We go west under the rusty iron girders in a passage barely wide enough and emerge in a pool backed by more undisturbed forest. I bear northwest briefly in the sharply narrower channel. In a few minutes a pair of northern harriers, first one and then the other, burst noisily from some hardwoods above me in a shudder of great wings, flying west in haste. I watch them beat farther upriver, but soon know I can go no farther myself. The river winds on, but there are only a few inches of water under *Merlin*'s hull now, and we ground out here and there. It is a chore to turn in this narrow spot, but turn we do, then just coast back north in the solitude.

I HAVE SAID much about Indians on these rivers because, though it is easy for many of us in the present to forget, the tribes were very much part of Maine river society as recently as a hundred years ago. And by "present" I mean as direct, visible participants in a number of communities. They are still very much with us today, of course, and their culture is enjoying a small renaissance, but their visible presence has much diminshed. It was not always so. As Fanny Hardy Eckstorm wrote: "A hundred years ago there were more Indians than whites in the town of Brewer, so my father said. That was in 1835. . . . From that time on for many years his associates were largely Indians." This reality prevailed in other Maine towns as well, particularly toward the north.

Of her paterfamilias, Eckstorm remembered: "His father's business was in part the buying of furs and articles made by Indians and all day long they came and went, buying and selling, begging and borrowing . . . they came on business or just for friendly conversation. . . . " In the early 1800s, Indians were allowed to set up camp in the community on "any unfenced site in the town that was suited to their manner of life and provided fresh water and firewood," according to Eckstorm's recollection.

When Thoreau came to Maine in the 1840s and 1850s, his river companions and guides were Penobscot. He disliked the laziness of a few, but generally appreciated and admired the resourcefulness and woods skills of the many. Indians were part of the lore of the North Woods, fished and hunted there, and yet were connected with the white world and were certainly a part of it as well. As whites paddled upriver and became involved in remote places, their instructors were often Indians who knew the countryside and whose methods of tracking, fishing, camping, and building watercraft and snowshoes were highly useful. A certain ironic contrast exists between those tribal peoples who traveled light in birch canoes, who camped in simple shelters, and who left little imprint on the land, and their white counterparts of today, who require a polluting, forty-two foot, diesel-powered "camper" with air conditioning.

I recall a time I came ashore at a camping area after paddling Moosehead Lake. I pitched my tent near the water in a relatively isolated spot, but not far away through the trees were row upon row of these giant "campers," generators idling, windows tightly shut against fresh air, air conditioners groaning, and their occupants hidden inside watching videos, while the idiotic flickering of television screens pierced the night air. This, too, was not always so.

Maine's Indians have been a continuous part of the state's maturing

Southwest of Bowdoinham on the broad Cathance

culture. Small signs appear that we may pay attention to them once again when they speak of the virtue of wild land. After all, Europeans adopted many aspects of the culture of Indian peoples in the 1800s. Such observances increased their prospects for survival. A few days before I set out on this trip, I listened to a lecture given by Barry Dana, then chief of the Penobscot Nation, who urged us all to protect Maine's recovering rivers and wild lands, much as Indian peoples have for decades. Dana equated the health of Maine's rivers with the health and worth of life itself. Perhaps this time we are listening.

I HAD BEEN watching the brilliant blue skies to the south, but now that I'm turned around I can see that black clouds have closed in behind me and that my downriver return to Bowdoinham is going to be a bit iffy. Where did that come from? As we move out into stretches of open marsh again, an intimidating roll of thunder announces itself from the west. A bar of massive black cloud arches from southwest to the northeast. I am still south of its cover and debate whether to try to outrun the storm or dally and wait until it passes. I move northward at a leisurely pace in the sun, watching the blackness ahead. Miles in the distance, great curtains of rain trail northeast.

Being on the water in a thunderstorm is not my notion of a party. I ought to have been more vigilant in keeping an eye on the weather behind me. Now, mid-journey on my return, I'm under the cloudbank, it's getting dark, and the sky has begun to sprinkle. More thunder and the occasional bolt of lightning erupt in the distance. Reluctant to get any closer to this enormous electrical machine, I peel off down a reedy channel to the west and look for a place to shelter. Making my way through tall cordgrass and drowned tree stumps, I come to a row of hemlocks that reaches out over the water, and shelter under its canopy. It's going to be a while. I wait and watch to see whether I'll need to get out of the boat entirely for safety. *Merlin* rides the water's edge while this great symphony of jagged lightning and tympanous thunder works its way toward the far northeast.

Waiting has its merits. I survey my nearby patch of shore and the marsh itself. I have a ringside seat for the passing light show like no other. Even the birds have gone quiet as we all mark time. In about twenty minutes the storm seems far enough away to chance continuing homeward. Birds take to the air again. I exit the side stream, and *Merlin* moves quickly north on the Cathance once more.

Pierced by shafts of horizontal sunlight as clouds begin to dismember, the sky slowly yields its dark overcast. Before long we are in the sun at last, but I get wet in the brief, sunny shower that trails the storm. The rain is warm and refreshing, and the emerging sun soon dries me off. In another half hour the bridge at Bowdoinham comes into view. Paddling steadily northeastward, I round a last broad bend and we enter the little harbor. And now I have done the navigable Cathance from stem to stern.

Day Eight

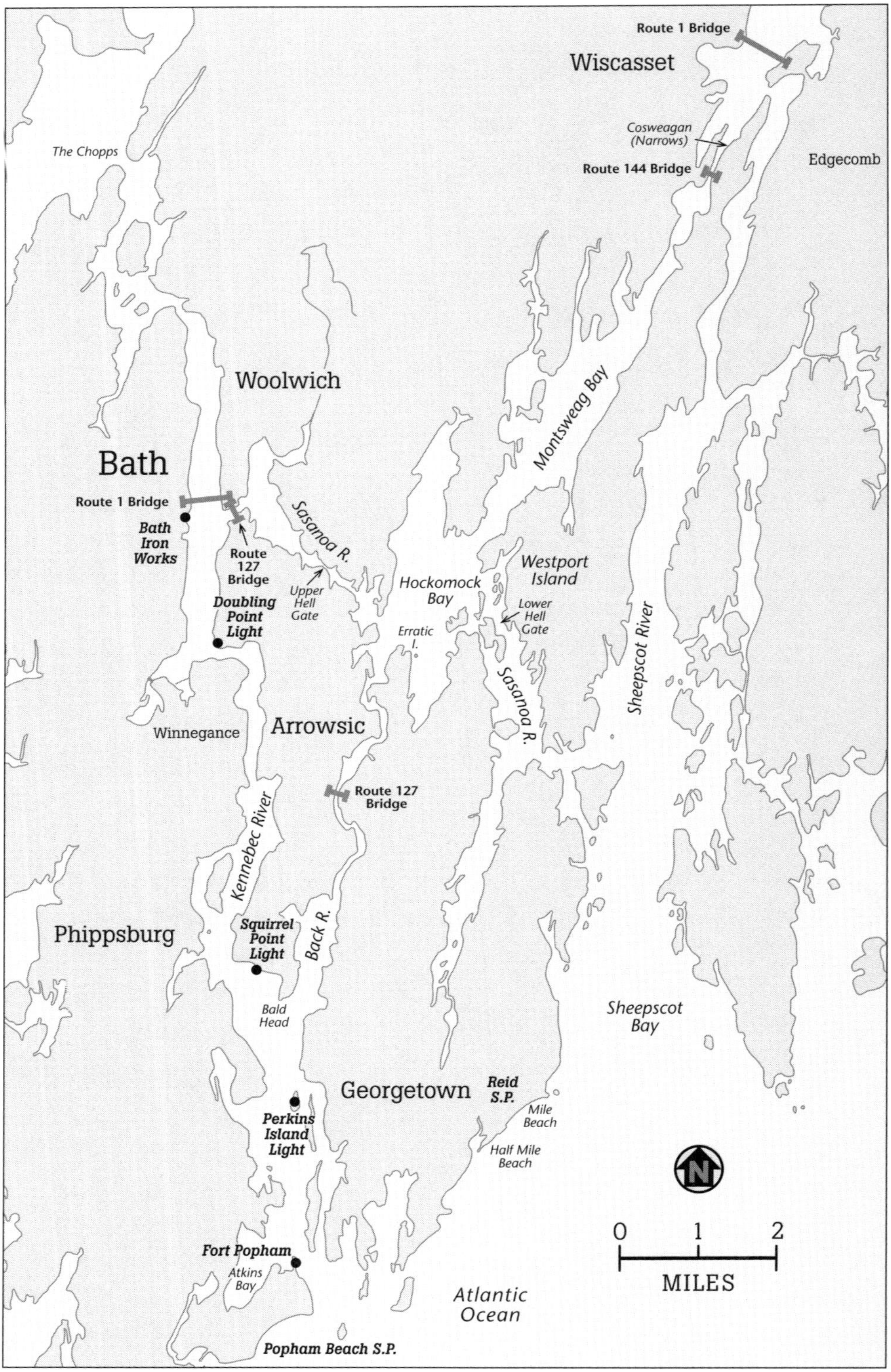
Route 1 Bridge
Wiscasset
Cosweagan
(Narrows)
Route 144 Bridge
Edgecomb
The Chopps
Woolwich
Montsweag Bay
Bath
Route 1 Bridge
Bath
Iron
Works
Route
127
Bridge
Sasanoa R.
Upper
Hell
Gate
Hockomock
Bay
Westport
Island
Lower
Hell
Gate
Doubling
Point
Light
Erratic
I.
Sasanoa R.
Sheepscot River
Winnegance
Arrowsic
Route 127
Bridge
Kennebec River
Phippsburg
Squirrel
Point
Light
Back R.
Bald
Head
Sheepscot
Bay
Georgetown
Reid
S.P.
Mile
Beach
Perkins
Island
Light
Half Mile
Beach
N
0
1
2
MILES
Fort Popham
Atkins
Bay
Atlantic
Ocean
Popham Beach S.P.

Wiscasset to the Lower Kennebec

[T]he coast doth abound with most convenient havens and harbours, full of singular islands fit for plantations. . . . The people are tractable (if they be not abused) to commerce and trade with all, and as yet have respect for us.

—Sir Ferdinando Gorges
In Praise of His Province to the North (1522)

It is five in the morning, not my favorite time of day. I'm not fond of six in the morning, either, but tolerate it on rare occasions—very rare. But here we are, slaves of the tide, I lowering *Merlin* into the water at the ramp in Wiscasset, the rest of the town wisely sound asleep, everything incredibly quiet except for my mumbling and splashing about. I wanted a certain kind of water and this is it. The tide, quite full and resting before departing for points south, won't begin to head in that direction for several hours, and that is essential.

I plan to gain the lower Kennebec, its saltwater precincts, by paddling southward a mile to the cleft at Cosweagan, leading into Montsweag Bay. From there I'll proceed into Hockomock Bay, a mixing bowl between Upper and Lower Hell Gates on the Sasanoa River. After crossing Hockomock Bay I'll enter the shallow northern reaches of the quiet Back River. I will need every inch of tide I can find to slide over clam flats and into the river's winding channel. Once in the Back, I will meander south and enter the lower Kennebec several miles above the point where it debouches into the Atlantic—the point, if you must know, where America got its start. (Don't get me started about Plymouth Rock again.)

Thinking my excursion to be roughly fifteen miles, I need to get over the shallow points before the tide turns and these rivers and bays begin disgorging their contents. Montsweag and Hockomock bays are expansive places when full, but less accommodating to the kayaker at low tide. The northern entrance to the Back is mere mud if you arrive at the wrong moment, so my day will be one of obedient punctuality. Anything less will leave *Merlin* and me very smelly, muddy travelers.

If you go straight oceanward from Wiscasset Bay, a left turn will lead down the Sheepscot on the east side of Westport Island and on toward the Atlantic, more or less directly. Instead, I make for a cut between wooded, ledgy banks, a narrows known by its Indian name, Cosweagan. This channel along Westport Island's west side is generally shallower than the Sheepscot, but businesslike enough to require warning notices on coastal charts about Cosweagan's dangerous currents. It is not a place to be when water levels are low and the channel is draining hard or filling rapidly. One can get pushed around with no room in which to be pushed around.

About a mile and a half south of Wiscasset Harbor, we enter the narrows. What little hint I have of approaching daylight disappears behind the dense growth bordering the channel. As I'd hoped, the high water allows plenty of maneuvering space and floats *Merlin* above the rough edges of what is a rather slim thread of water here at low tide. We float through comfortably, the current relaxed, and pass under the high bridge that connects the mainland with Westport Island.

The air is cool—almost cold, given the chilly water temperature and the hour—the air clear and free of early fog. Staying in the channel that hugs the land, we coast along the mainland shore and soon reach the opening that leads into broad, shallow Montsweag Bay. It is a pretty bay, not much built up. Its length runs north and south, and it is shallow enough so that a good part of its surface becomes open to clamming at low tide. I have occasionally walked The Nature Conservancy's Montsweag Preserve at the top of the bay where I have seen lone figures, backs bent, harvesting clams between tides out beyond Chewonki Neck. Montsweag is really two bays, inner and outer, one long and thin, the other more round and expansive. I have no time this morning to ride up into the inner catchment. With one eye on the clock, I keep moving, riding the flat water the length of the bay and paddling steadily.

Not far below the mouth of the inner bay, I pass Phipps Point on Westport Island and enter Hockomock Bay, which separates the point from the mainland. Except for the occasional house or cottage, the shore is wooded and dark. Nearly nine miles below Wiscasset, Hockomock Bay, though not on the Atlantic, handles a lot of tidal water. Some arrives from the north as the river drains via Montsweag, some from the west via the Sasanoa, and more from rangy Knubble Bay and Goose Rock Passage to the south and from the Back River. When the tide is working, small craft feel the tug of strong currents here in one direction or another. Like Cosweagan, Hockomock Bay is a place better navigated at slack tide.

Dorcas Miller's indispensable *Kayaking the Maine Coast* spends several paragraphs warning of the hazards to kayakers at Upper and Lower Hell Gates on the Sasanoa River, the northwest and southeast entries to lower Hockomock Bay. When current moves through either of these points of compression, flow rates exceed headway speed for all but the strongest kayakers, so controlling the direction of one's boat becomes quite difficult. In particular, Upper Hell Gate can be a nasty place to be caught when water is moving rapidly through it. The upper Sasanoa River connects with the Kennebec opposite Bath, adding further to the unpredictable crosspatch of current that governs these channels. Ledge abounds, and in summer, herds of power craft shuttle through in all directions, requiring a great deal of caution.

Despite its occasional challenges, Hockomock delights the eye—or at least what I can see of it in the early light. Setting my sights due southwest, I steer *Merlin* across the bay, passing several diminutive islands and stroking toward the mouth of the Back River. The Back can be hard to find, its entrance lodged in a wooded cove floored with tidal mud just west of Flying Point. Today's early start was prompted mainly by the need to get over that mud on a full head of tide, and that keeps me looking ahead and paddling steadily now. Keeping one eye cocked for approaching traffic coming down the Sasanoa from the west, I also look eastward, but see nothing. What does register is the push of

Inland marsh, Georgetown Island

the Sasanoa. Its currents cross the bay (the bay is in reality a widening of the river), and it has begun to move a little. A light breeze tumbles out of the northwest here.

Approaching the south shore of Hockomock, I am first tempted to enter its southern cavity, Hall Bay. A few minutes of comparing observations and squinting into the distance confirms this is not what I am looking for. Hall Bay dead-ends in a marsh on Georgetown Island. (The Appalachian Mountain Club's Beal Island campsite is near here, just to the east.) I paddle farther west, around Flying Point, and then finally to the opening of the Back River. I sight on a green channel buoy, and, leaning south, in we go. *Merlin* and I will ride this narrow channel southward for about five miles.

I navigate the divide between two large islands, Georgetown on the left, Arrowsic on the right. The Back is, then, a river that never directly touches the mainland, a conduit only for distributing the tide and carrying it back oceanward in this incredible mix-up of rivers, bays, marshes, flats, and islands. From beginning to end, the Back is a river all at sea. Georgetown is an island community, though not much thought of as such because you can drive onto it. Its two majestic sand beaches at Reid State park are, I think, the finest in Maine. Popham Beach, where I hope to land later in the day, comes a close second.

THIS NECK of the woods has its own history. Europeans visited Maine's shores for centuries before the "Pilgrims" were said to have "begun" America in 1620. Sailing under the banner of Francis I of France, Giovanni da Verrazano cruised along this coast in 1524. It is likely he was preceded by Portuguese fishermen and certainly by those Norse who landed farther north in 1011. English merchant voyagers under Captain George Waymouth landed and made contact with Abenakis near here in 1605. Champlain sailed in these waters in the spring of 1605, too. The journal of Welshman Captain Robert Davies records the expedition of George Popham and Rawleigh Gilbert in 1607 to establish the colony that would carry Popham's name to the present.

When the Popham group reached these shores, local Indians were warned by their sachems to stay clear of the white arrivals. Speaking through these sachems, their god, Tanto, urged them not to associate with or live near the English, perhaps wisely. According to local historians, when Gilbert had come ashore two years earlier, he apparently offended natives by refusing the gifts they offered.

Curiosity proved stronger than these injunctions or offenses for some natives, who mixed freely with members of the Popham Colony and sometimes proved helpful to the fragile little outpost. Writing much later, in May 1754, Captain Samuel Goodwin noted the useful cooperation of local Indians even as hostilities continued in pockets up and down the major rivers, but at the time of the Popham Colony, this on-again, off-again connection had deteriorated, with growing mistrust on both sides.

There is a persistent story, probably apocryphal, that is indicative of the kind of abuse the Popham band allegedly found amusing. In 1607 or 1608, a small group of native people, interested in what was going on at the fledgling settlement, appeared one day at Popham. They asked questions about a small ship's cannon that had been set up on the shore. It will be remembered that, at this time, native peoples had little or no experience of gunpowder and firearms generally. They were cheerfully promised a demonstration by the amused British. The tribesmen were told to line up, one man behind the other, with the first man facing the cannon's muzzle. The Popham men primed and loaded the cannon and handed the lead Indian the igniter. He was told to put fire to the touch hole when he wished to see the cannon operate, and, the story records, he did so without question.

The Popham Colony failed, some going back to England at once, others overwintering on Damariscove Island. The following spring all those still alive fled.

The French attempted a more constructive relationship with Abenakis farther above on the Kennebec. Jesuit Father Gabriel Dreuillettes arrived up-river at Norridgewock, probably in 1646, and began a Catholic settlement at Old Point where they developed trustworthy connections with local tribesmen. Still, hostility spread as native peoples began to understand that white settlement meant their inevitable displacement. Despite growing rancor, the English continued trading relations with Abenakis along the Kennebec, though they insisted that those Indians who had obtained rifles give them up as a condition of trade. As relations worsened after 1675, they finally withdrew their truck house on the river. The French continued to enjoy harmonious relations with the tribes they contacted, and even assumed some of their ways.

Maine chronicler Louise Dickinson Rich, in *The Kennebec River*, described the various incentives the English offered tribes along the river to convert to Protestantism. Father Sebastian Râle had by then taken over the Norridgewock settlement and enjoyed the continuing support and allegiance of those Abenakis around him. The English found his influence in the region unacceptable and hoped to break Râle's Catholic hold on the tribes. They imported a preacher who built a church to conduct mass conversions, but no Indian would enter it. After the English burned the Norridgewock settlement in 1722, Râle and his followers rebuilt. The English came upriver again in August 1724, two hundred strong, and destroyed the village a second time. During this raid, one Jacques, a half-breed in English pay, murdered Father Râle.

Years later, as I have mentioned, the British erected Fort Halifax on this river near Winslow in 1754, increasing the sense of threat felt by natives living nearby. Frequent raids and enforcement patrols by the British gradually reduced the power of the tribal Kennebecs along the river, and the Penobscots became more dominant in their settlements to the northeast. As late as November 1755, Massachusetts Governor Spencer Phips offered fifty pounds each for Indian prisoners or scalps taken from the Penobscot nation, despite the fact that Penobscots had been generally friendly to the British, warning them of impending attacks by other tribes. Both the English and French attempted to enlist natives in the forces they deployed, but were only rarely successful.

When Benedict Arnold came up the Kennebec in the autumn of 1775, settlers on Georgetown Island welcomed him. He moored his ship somewhere close to where I make headway today and waited for his expedition to catch up with him. One of Arnold's ships got lost as his comical little fleet attempted to organize itself in the lower Kennebec. I fancy that the wayward schooner came up a distance on the Back, probably on a less favorable tide than today's, before it found its way again into the Kennebec. The Georgetown boys were committed revolutionaries, freshly back from some interesting skirmishes in Boston. Some, we are told, joined Arnold's force.

THE BACK RIVER, portions of which I had seen and admired from the land, is wonderful to travel. It's as pretty a river as one is likely to find in New England, wandering through unsettled marsh and woodland, close to bigger rivers, but with a quiet, often glassy personality of its own. I give *Merlin* a heading, setting a course between points of intruding shore. There are ospreys here, a variety of ducks and gulls, and probably an eagle aerie, though I see none today. These and other birds fly above the wider, open stretches of water. The Back burrows through elevated bogs of ancient sediment for nearly a mile. Here the river has scoured a channel for itself, and we are often down in this shallow cleft between high banks of compressed vegetation. I paddle southwest silently, taking in the sounds of the woods, gazing ahead to my expected rendezvous with the lower Kennebec. After three days on bigger rivers, I find this protected, little-used stream to be a salutary tonic. I am loathe to dip the paddle or to break the silence.

With a breeze drifting out of the southwest, I fall to thinking about Thoreau again. What would we do without him and Emerson, the two seminal American thinkers who did not extol acquisition and destruction? They who saw in exploration an opportunity for husbandry and quiet engagement, not pillage. When I was on the Concord, I went to the reproduction of Thoreau's small cabin nearby. Living deliberately, taking the woods on its own terms, understanding the wider world from a local outpost: Thoreau's dicta and the very sentiments that had brought me to these rivers.

Henry had no interest in going somewhere distant merely for the sake of going. Novelty, in the sense that most Americans today are drugged by it, was not a dominant motive for him. He looked for continuities in his own region, feeling always that most of us are half-blind to the nature that surrounds us. As I wrote on the day I began this trip, he was fascinated by the complexities of place, and the places he experienced were mainly in his native Northeast. All of this was in the name of looking around, an appreciation of overlooked terrain in a region he sensed was representative of what geography and community might most favorably be. He once wrote, "The most familiar sheet of water viewed from a new hilltop, yields a novel and unexpected pleasure. When we have traveled a few miles, we do not recognize the profiles even of the hills which overlook our native village, and perhaps no man is quite familiar with the horizon as seen from the hill nearest to his house. . . . It is an important epoch when a man who has always lived on the east side of the mountain and seen it in the west, travels round and sees it in the east."

Thoreau seems to have been born with a geographic sense and a burning need to journalize about it. His ability to anatomize even the merest details of the woods and rivers he followed is nearly without precedent. One thinks of Gilbert White's *Natural History of Selborne*, but Thoreau is somehow more interesting or motivating. Thoreau told us not only how the natural world appears, but always what the natural world *means*. He also possessed the carpenter's eye and built not only his Walden cabin and the dory *Musketaquid*, but worked with his father to build a house in Concord. He made a good part of his living as a surveyor and fulminated against the outrageously poor property and community maps he encountered, revising as he went. A man who aggressively shunned any kind of formal worship, he wrote incessantly about matters of the soul and spirit. A ride on the Concord and Merrimack with him is as often about such things as it is about rivers or places. Seldom traveling outside of New England, he found a world to interest him within striking distance. His God was alive in the natural world. And here I am, as if at his behest, paddling southwest and enjoying still another "bran-new" stream.

PASSING TINY CROW ISLAND, I reach the edge of the Kennebec, the Back suddenly seeming small. The Kennebec, too, is at flood, and in the warming sun I am content to drift a little. *Merlin* passes between two red buoys in about forty-five feet of water and gains the bigger river by submerged Parker Flats. It remains to be seen what the Kennebec currents will exact during these last few miles. I hope to spend the final moments of my week of rivers at a slow pace, not a gallop. As we edge into midstream, the Kennebec is brimming and relatively quiet. We turn downriver and head for the sea. I guess that another hour and a half, maybe two if I dawdle, will get us down to Popham.

The river becomes broader here, with any number of back coves, inlets, and marsh borders. Upstream is Squirrel Point Light, opposite Phippsburg, one of three lights and many beacons on the lower river. Farther above us and out of sight now is Doubling Point Light, guarding Fiddler Reach. (Depending on how inclusive you want to be, there are, perhaps, six lights connected to the Kennebec below Bath. Besides Squirrel and Doubling, one might count the Kennebec Range, Perkins Island, and Pond Island lights. Some would also include Seguin Light, a prominent sentry off the river's mouth.)

In winter, U.S. Coast Guard ice cutters travel upriver here, breaking ice as far as the bridges at Richmond or Gardiner. I find the ability to get boats of that size through Fiddler Reach and other tight spots impressive. The narrowest places in the lower Kennebec seem to be its deepest also, so draft is not necessarily a problem. Making the turns must be challenging, however. Aegis destroyers built at Bath Iron Works are brought up and down this section of river, too, and, given their length, hauling them through the reach demands a bit of calculation. Sliding such large ships past Doubling Point and then down the Kennebec's very narrow throat near Winnegance amounts to serious piloting.

PHIPPSBURG FRONTS not only on the Kennebec but also, one channel over, on the lower reaches of the New Meadows River. Along that stretch of river are a number of small islands that from time to time have been places of refuge for those fed up with the mainland. Maine poet Holman Day, in a 1909 *Harper's Magazine* piece entitled "The Queer Folk of the Maine Coast," gave readers the lives of the inhabitants of Maine's little visited islands, but none at such length as those who inhabited the Phippsburg island of Malaga. Among the collection of ragtag river islands that have been home to small groups of those disaffected enough to move offshore, few have earned reputations as conflicted or unsavory as Malaga.

This island off Phippsburg's west shore is small and flat and was rarely home to more than fifty souls. "As a no man's land Malaga has more striking peculiarities than any other island alongshore," Day noted. "There are about fifty persons on it of all grades of negro blood, and most of them descendants of a runaway slave who came and hid there more years ago than any man about there remembers. These people form a strange clan." At one point, Malaga recognized one of its own as king.

There were probably whites of uncertain provenance on the island also, and Day sensed that not all was well: "They have married and intermarried until the trespass on consanguinity has produced its usual lamentable effects," he concluded. Day wrote that an island of simpletons had resulted, people who could not take care of themselves. "They are as near to be children of nature as it is possible for people to be who are only a stone's throw from the mainland and civilization," he said.

This fecklessness showed itself most troublingly in winter, when the collection of poor huts and odd buildings that peppered the island often went unheated, the wind whistling through cracks in the walls. "Winter after winter," wrote Day, "through all the years, they have shivered and starved, but never does November find a woodpile on Malaga, nor a week's supply of food in reserve." Somehow, the improvident community survived, and stories are told of how much Malaga people loved their island despite the hardship. Charity came from shore occasionally in the form of food and old clothing, but these gifts did little to elevate islanders to a better standard of living. They fished and went clamming in summer, and some of the island's women worked on mainland farms. However, to those like Day who disapproved of Malaga's way of life, the money earned was squandered on silly things that did not mitigate the harshness of poverty or the bitterness of winter.

More recent investigations of life on Malaga have painted a different picture, one of people who were self-reliant, respected, and skilled enough to earn their way as commercial fishermen. I have read accounts of Malaga men taking their catches to Portland markets, where the islanders were well received and viewed as honest and hardworking. There are bits of evidence, even in Day's own prose, that suggest Malaga people were not necessarily much worse off than the hermetic souls living on other Maine islands at the time. Except in the coastal enclaves of the wealthy from elsewhere, Maine has never been an easy, opulent place in which to engineer survival, and Malaga people appear to have been similar to other rural residents who were leading hardscrabble lives in a cold place.

But it could not go on. Phippsburg and nearby Harpswell saw their poor roll accounts swell as attempts to assist Malagans increased. The state legislature was unsympathetic. Still more were horrified at thoughts of island residents living in what they assumed was pleasant debauchery. A good deal of garden-variety racism figured in the matter, as well. The State of Maine, perhaps more moved by suspicions of miscegenation than charity, bought the windswept island from its absentee owners in February 1912 for four hundred dollars. Feckless or frugal, clever or misguided, Malaga and her people had become unacceptable both to the surrounding communities and to politicians eager to display their vigilance. The order came down from Augusta that everyone was to be removed from the island no later than June 1912. Though there were certainly more desperate island populations along the Maine coast, this one was to be disbanded as an embarrassment. Malaga's residents were ferried ashore, some weeping. The state provided a small stipend to each family. Some went to live on local farms; a few were institutionalized; some settled on shore; still others disappeared. Despite the pleas of those who would live there, buildings on the island were torn down or burned to the ground, and the unconventional river settlement ended.

TAKING THE RIGHT channel around Perkins Island, *Merlin* and I coast down the west shore of Marr Island, leisurely working our way south. Perkins Island Light catches my eye as I make the turn. Shallow Todd Bay lies to the left, now flooded. Pulling westward, we rejoin the main channel just above Dix Island, and I spend a few minutes looking around shallow Wyman Bay, coming in just above Cox Head. Even at full water, this is a place of little draft, and I do not push *Merlin* far into what will later become a broad mudflat as the tide ebbs. It is surprising how quickly depths here go from near zero to as

Reid State Park, Georgetown, near the outlet of the Kennebec and Back rivers

much as seventy-five feet off Cox Head; where the full force of the current works, there is depth.

The morning has worn itself out, the air only slightly warmer now, and fall-like. I watch for Shag Rock buoy, and we maneuver to stay right of it and the slender north-south expanse of Long Island. Atkins Bay appears to my right, and far ahead I can see the thin spit of land that is the site of Fort Popham. Off to the southeast I spy the open Atlantic. Beyond, behind a screen of islands, the tallest lighthouse in eastern America stands on Seguin Island. The light was built for less than seven thousand dollars in 1795, during the last days of the administration of George Washington. It was upgraded in 1842 and the tower augmented in 1857. The current beacon is 188 feet above the level of surrounding seas. The light became an essential feature of navigation for ships approaching the Kennebec or lower Sheepscot. It is a seemly looking outpost, a coastal landmark.

Moving forward toward the sea, I soon need to revise my forecast. The wind has turned, and I feel the breeze coming upriver from the Atlantic; nothing summery about this. The air is now cool and getting just plain cold. I pull a windbreaker from the deck bungees and put it on. The smell of salt air builds. I watch as the sea gradually becomes part of my front yard. Rather suddenly, I am finished, my week on the water winding down, and I look for a place to bring *Merlin* ashore. The best decision favors a landing on the crescent-shaped beach by Fort Popham in front of the town library. I maneuver for a gentle pull ashore. It will soon be time to take stock, and, again, Henry Thoreau had anticipated my own mental drift as I near the shingle.

Thoreau mused in his journal: "It is easier to discover such a new world as Columbus did, than to go within one fold of this which we appear to know so well; the land is lost sight of, the compass varies, and mankind mutiny; and still history accumulates rubbish before the portals of nature." Speaking for myself, I have chipped away a little at that blindness during these river days. With Henry's urging, I began to see more clearly what I had thought familiar. There can be no substitute for going and looking, I think. Henry continued, "Men nowhere, east or west, live yet a natural life, round which the vine clings, and which the elm willingly shadows. Man would desecrate it by his touch, and so the beauty of the world remains veiled to him."

Well, Henry, I beg to report that beauty still abides along those back roads and quiet Maine rivers where our human fumbling has not sullied the ground. Moreover, the view is even more gratifying from water than land—but then, you know that. Taking in dozens of tranquil, pleasant, and, yes, beautiful river places during my wanderings, I have observed, close up, those several neighborhoods where the country's earliest history played itself out, too. I make my way ashore thinking on the subject of balance, some sort of equilibrium between the marketplace and the natural world that we are in danger of losing. Nature and history do well enough together if left alone, out of the marketplace.

I have arrived at a certain comfort, having seen that so much formerly exploited territory is reverting to woods, unpeopled streamsides, and healthy waters. The slow, steady effort of many Maine people has made of these once recklessly used rivers and their surroundings a better place. With some further tending, they will be a credit to Maine indefinitely. My journey has been a kind of confirmation, too, the view from the river filling in details, yielding a different sense of this part of the world, linking ideas that can only be realized on water. I have rarely invested eight days so well.

Having loaded *Merlin* on the car, I turn away from the river one more time. I will come back, of course. There will be other rivers and other days. For now, I head homeward, musing on Thoreau's farewells as he and his brother returned from their sojourn on the Concord and the Merrimack rivers: "Thus, thoughtfully, we were rowing homeward to find some autumnal work to do, and help on the revolution of the seasons. Perhaps nature would condescend to make use of us even without our knowledge, as when we scatter her seeds in our walks, and carry burrs and cockles in our clothes from field to field. . . . I am glad to find that nature wears so well. The landscape is indeed something real, and solid, and sincere, and I have not put my foot through it yet."

Good man, Henry.

Acknowledgments and Late Reading

These travels would have been wearying if done in anything other than a well-designed and well-constructed boat. Thanks are due to Tom Derrer, designer-owner, and Joe Audrey, general manager, at Eddyline Kayaks in Burlington, Washington. *Merlin* was a gentleman and boon companion in all our days on the rivers and bodes well to be so on more rivers to come. All kayaks should be this good.

Thanks are also due to Karin Womer, senior editor at Down East Books, for transforming another wandering tale into the book before you. One of those invisible people who make the finished book possible and, the author hopes, enjoyable.

IF ONE LIKES reading that pertains to the rivers traveled, there is a lot of it.

Ever a readable and comprehensive look at Maine's history, *Maine: The Pine Tree State from Prehistory to the Present,* by Richard Judd, Edwin Churchill, and Joel Eastman is always informative.

Bruce Bourque, of the Maine State Museum, captures the reader's willing hours with the many interesting glimpses of early Indian life provided in *Twelve Thousand Years: American Indians in Maine.* The classic introduction to tribal life in the Northeast has long been Frank G. Speck's *Penobscot Man.* Ruth Holmes Whitehead's *Stories from the Six Worlds* is just one of several works in which she retells classic Northeastern Indian stories. Howard Russell's *Indian New England Before the Mayflower* is evidence enough of the dynamic Indian way of life here along Maine's rivers or elsewhere in New England before whites "discovered" America. A pleasnat collection of Micmac stories is *On the Trail of Elder Brother* by Michael Runningwolf and Patricia Clark Smith.

William Hutchinson Rowe has written the important *The Maritime History of Maine* and Garnet Eskew's *Cradle of Ships: A History of Bath Iron Works* chronicles the complete story of shipbuilding on the lower Kennebec.

Jennie G. Everson's *Tidewater Ice of the Kennebec River* is a marvelous illustrated history of the frozen-water business on the Kennebec that reached out to the world.

Elizabeth Coatsworth has written widely on Maine, and in various essays, including those in *Maine Memories*, there are glimpses of Maine rivers. Arthur R. Macdougall Jr. gave us many stories of fabled Maine guide Dud Dean and his fishing exploits on the Kennebec, none better so than in *Where Flows the Kennebec.* Robert P.T. Coffin's *Kennebec: Cradle of Americans* is a pleasant general introduction to the river's history. *Land of the Kennebec* by Stanwood and Margaret Gilman provides a lot of local interest, and Mary Calvert's *Dawn Over the Kennebec* tells much about the river through its major figures and history. Louise Dickinson Rich, among her many writings about Maine, found time for *The Kennebec River,* and Maine newspaperman and author Bill Caldwell discourses engagingly about settlers and commerce along Maine's big rivers in his popular *Rivers of Fortune.* Roger F. Duncan's *Coastal Maine: A Maritime History* is also interesting reading.

For those interested in Henry David Thoreau's visits to Maine, there are his wide-ranging *Journals,* his great essay *The Maine Woods,* and his discursive remarks on paddling a network of rivers in *A Week on the Concord and Merrimack Rivers.* Parker Huber's excellent *The Wildest Country: A Guide to Thoreau's Maine* will put the Concordman's visits here in perspective.